Encompassing

Encompassing

Practical Applications Through Simulation

Jean-François Richard, Robert C. Marshall, and Chaohai Shen

The MIT Press
Cambridge, Massachusetts
London, England

The MIT Press
Massachusetts Institute of Technology
77 Massachusetts Avenue, Cambridge, MA 02139
mitpress.mit.edu

The MIT Press would like to thank the anonymous peer reviewers who provided comments on drafts of this book. The generous work of academic experts is essential for establishing the authority and quality of our publications. We acknowledge with gratitude the contributions of these otherwise uncredited readers.

This book was set in Times New Roman by Westchester Publishing Services. Printed and bound in the United States of America.

Library of Congress Cataloging-in-Publication Data

Names: Richard, Jean-François, 1943- author
Title: Encompassing : practical applications through simulation /
Jean-François Richard, Robert C. Marshall, and Chaohai Shen.
Description: Cambridge, Massachusetts : The MIT Press, [2025] | Includes
bibliographical references and index.
Identifiers: LCCN 2024049510 (print) | LCCN 2024049511 (ebook) | ISBN
9780262553094 paperback | ISBN 9780262384063 pdf | ISBN 9780262384070 epub
Subjects: LCSH: Econometrics | Equations, Simultaneous
Classification: LCC HB139 .R52 2025 (print) | LCC HB139 (ebook) |
DDC 330.01/5195–dc23/eng/20250326
LC record available at https://lccn.loc.gov/2024049510
LC ebook record available at https://lccn.loc.gov/2024049511

10 9 8 7 6 5 4 3 2 1

EU Authorised Representative: Easy Access System Europe, Mustamäe tee 50, 10621 Tallinn, Estonia | Email: gpsr.requests@easproject.com

In loving memory of Tanguy

Contents

Acronyms

ALP	Alaska Lumber and Pulp Company
BMR	Baldwin, Marshall and Richard
CH	Chong and Hendry
CME	conditional mean encompassing
CPE	complete parametric encompassing
CRN	common random number
DGM	Dhaene, Gouriéroux and Monfort
DGP	data generation process
DSGE	Dynamic Stochastic General Equilibrium
GET	generalized encompassing test
GMM	generalized method of moments
GUM	General Unrestricted Model
HMR	Hendry, Mizon and Richard
IDL	Idaho Department of Lands
KLIC	Kullback-Leibler Information Criterion
KPC	Ketchikan Pulp Co.
MBF	one thousand board feet
MC	Monte Carlo
ML	maximum likelihood
MSFE	mean square forecast errors
MSM	method of simulated moments
OLS	ordinary least squares
RBLC	Reid Bros. Logging Co.
RMSE	root mean squared errors
SET	score encompassing test
SURE	seemingly unrelated regression equations
TDC	Timber Data Company
USFS	United States Forest Service
WET	Wald encompassing test
WTP	willingness to pay

Preface

Marshall and Richard are full coauthors on the entirety of the book. Shen's predominant contribution was chapter 6, where he is a full coauthor with Marshall and Richard.

As a guide for applied micro researchers interested strictly in understanding our main points and how they might implement simulation-based encompassing in their work, chapters 1, 6, and 7 are essential. Chapter 2 is quite important as well, especially sections 2.3, 2.4, 2.5, and 2.9. For those familiar with the method of simulated moments, only section 4.3 is recommended in chapter 4. In chapter 5, we encourage careful attention to sections 5.2 and 5.4. A table of acronyms follows the table of contents.

The book began as a paper that consisted of chapter 6 and small parts of chapters 2, 4, and 5. It became clear from the refereeing process that the page limitations of a journal article made it impossible to explain both our contributions regarding encompassing and the details of the timber auction application.

Richard acknowledges his long-standing collaboration with David Hendry, Grayham Mizon, and Jean-Pierre Florens, who co-authored with him several papers that formalized a theoretical concept of encompassing in econometrics some 35 years ago. David and Jean-Pierre also offered insightful comments on the novel application-oriented concept of encompassing presented in this book.

We thank participants to a GREMAQ (Marseille) seminar for their suggestions. With regard to the data processing for the application in chapter 6, we are grateful to Alexandra Kaminsky, Luc Lallement, Arazi Lubis, Margaret Sabelhaus, Jinzi Sheng, and especially Charles Horgan. Noah Lyman helped with several useful discussions regarding the method of simulated moments (MSM). We thank Doug McDonald for numerous helpful interactions regarding the timber industry, timber auctions, and our data. In addition, we are grateful to the Idaho Department of Lands (IDL) staff for completing public information requests from us and for comments during two presentations of chapter 6.

Finally, on a personal note. Marshall is grateful for the patience and support of his wife, Anne. Richard greatly benefited from the love of his wife, Colette (even though she had other plans for his retirement). Shen is indebted to his parents, Jianyi and Yunfei, for their support.

1

Introduction

We begin with an obvious observation—an empirical researcher should not stop once they have estimated an empirical model that produces the results they like. At a minimum, numerous tests of the model should be conducted. In addition, the model should be evaluated relative to serious alternative models. This is the essence of the econometric concept of encompassing, which will be a focus of this book.[1]

Many economic theories are about the primitives of firms or individuals, but the observed data is about outcomes. For example, in an auction context, economic theories describe how firms or individuals formulate valuations for an item being sold and how those valuations map into bids, but the observed data will almost exclusively be about outcomes—bidder participation and realized prices. However, the economic theories allow us to formulate empirical models from which we can, through simulations, generate bidder participation and realized prices. Simulations of these relatively complex environments permit us to compare a model, in detail, to a serious alternative model.

Obviously, empirical models inevitably rely upon simplifying assumptions. It is also frequently the case that key components of agents' behavior might not be observable. Last but not least, empirical models typically include exogenous variables whose generating process is, by definition, left unspecified (the critical role of exogeneity assumptions will be discussed in section 2.8). Therefore, it makes absolutely no sense to require an empirical researcher in economics, who is investigating a nontrivial phenomenon, to have identified the underlying process that produced the data, referred to as the data generation process (DGP).

> "All models are approximations. Assumptions, whether implied or clearly stated, are never exactly true. *All models are wrong, but some models are useful.*"[2]

This raises a fundamental question: How does one determine if a given model is more useful than alternatives with regard to the researcher's objectives?

A compelling answer is provided by the extraordinary success over centuries of an implicit "progressive" research strategy in science, which consists of analyzing whether a "new" model can account for (encompass) successes and, foremost, failures of earlier models. We argue that this encompassing principle is the most compelling way to assess the usefulness of one's preferred model and, in case of failure, to suggest further improvements of that model, if at all possible, in view of inherent data limitations.

Foremost, we provide a simulation-based operational version of encompassing that is widely applicable to serious empirical models under the minimal requirement that these be amenable to Monte Carlo (MC) simulations.

Construction of a Model

We assume that a researcher has produced a best or preferred model according to whatever criteria were part of their modeling strategy. In this book, we are not suggesting a universally accepted set of criteria. We are assuming that the researcher has been thoughtful and deliberate in the model construction. Thus we are at the stage where a researcher is ready to use the model for policy interpretations. It is essential to emphasize that if the model satisfies all the criteria that were used during its construction, then this does not imply the eventual soundness of the model for policy analyses. No matter how thoughtful and deliberate a researcher has been in constructing an empirical model of a serious economic phenomenon, that model is not the DGP! What is critically needed is confronting the model with serious alternative models. These could be models developed by other researchers or special cases of one's own model derived under alternative assumptions.

In this book, we introduce an econometric version of encompassing that (1) conforms to its seminal interpretation of "accounting for" and (2) is fully operational in serious empirical applications under the minimal (sensible) requirement that the models under consideration be amenable to MC simulations.

Overview of Encompassing

The concept of encompassing formalizes a principle that is widely accepted in the methodology of sciences (see, e.g., Popper, 1963 and Lakatos, 1978)–namely, that one's "latest" model, M_1, should be able to account for ("encompass") the findings of alternative models, such as M_2.

However, a finding that M_1 encompasses M_2 should not be interpreted as evidence that M_1 is the DGP. Again, it should be understood, as it is in other scientific disciplines, that M_1 will *never* be the DGP.

As reviewed at length in chapter 2, a formal econometric definition of "parametric encompassing" was introduced some forty years ago and has since been generalized in a number of ways (obviously, researchers had applied informal versions of encompassing well before that time). The defining characteristics of this original parametric encompassing are as follows:

1. Its initial motivation was largely theoretical, aimed at providing a unified framework for a wide range of existing test statistics, and it has unquestionably been very successful in this respect.
2. To achieve that theoretical objective, it relies on an asymptotic loglikelihood-based approach that provides unambiguous definitions for the relevant key concepts.
3. Relatedly, the derivation of the relevant limiting distributions is generally far too complicated to be routinely implemented for serious empirical applications.
4. Empirical economists don't have the luxury to wait for currently unavailable data. As in the case in sciences, they have to reach policy conclusions based upon available information at the time (obviously, they would want to rely upon inference techniques that are statistically sound, and asymptotic theory can provide useful guidelines in this respect).
5. Maximum likelihood (ML) estimation is generally far too complicated to be routinely applied to most serious empirical applications. While this might be resolved by future computing advances (e.g., quantum computers), there remains a more fundamental issue. Specifically, as discussed further in chapter 3, while ML is theoretically efficient under correct specfciation, it also lacks robustness against unavoidable specification errors. In an important sense, ML lies at a corner of the efficiency/robustness trade-off. In this respect, moment-based estimation procedures such as the generalized method of moments (GMM) and the method of simulated moments (MSM) are inherently less efficient but more robust than ML, as discussed further in chapter 4. These are the two key reasons why GMM, and foremost MSM, are widely applied in major applications.

Alternative Versions of Encompassing

For ease of presentation, assume that we have estimated both M_1 and M_2 as $\hat{M}_1 = M_1(\hat{\alpha})$ and $\hat{M}_2 = M_2(\hat{\delta})$. All three versions of encompassing presented in chapter 2 share a common interpretation of encompassing, that of testing whether $\hat{M}_1$ can account for $\hat{\delta}$ (or any other statistic of interest associated with $\hat{M}_2$). Specifically, the common encompassing statistic of interest is the encompassing difference $\hat{\phi} = \hat{\delta} - \delta_1(\hat{\alpha})$, where $\delta_1(\hat{\alpha})$ denotes the predicted value of $\hat{\delta}$ under $\hat{M}_1$. The differences among the three versions of encompassing lie in the selection of the distribution used to assess the statistical significance of $\hat{\phi}$:

1. Under the approach associated with Hendry, Mizon, and Richard (HMR), the relevant distribution is that of $\hat{\phi}$, given $M_1(\alpha)$. Obviously, since α is unknown, it will be replaced by $\hat{\alpha}$ in the final expression of the resulting encompassing test statistics.
2. Under the approach associated with Dhaene, Gouriéroux, and Monfort (DGM), the relevant distribution is that of $\hat{\phi}$, given $M_0(\theta)$, where $M_0(\theta)$ denotes the unknown DGP. Since $M_0(\theta)$ is unknown, the computation of DGM encompassing test statistics is quite complicated and will not be discussed in this book. On the other hand, as discussed in section 2.4.2, the DGM approach is important for highlighting the implications of the fact that the data is generated by the (unattainable) DGP, not by $M_1(\alpha)$.
3. Under the approach proposed in section 2.4.3, the relevant distribution is that of $\hat{\delta}$, given $M_1(\hat{\alpha})$; that is, $\hat{\alpha}$ is kept fixed at its finite sample estimated value. As we shall see, that assumption considerably simplifies the computation of the relevant test statistics. Foremost, by being based upon $M_1(\hat{\alpha})$, as estimated from the available data and from the corresponding finite sample distribution of $\hat{\phi}$, we believe that our approach is closest to how encompassing has been successfully applied in sciences for a very long time.

Notation

The finite sample version of encompassing we present below differs from the HMR and DGM asymptotic versions. To avoid any eventual confusion, we shall use acronyms for the HMR and DGM versions of encompassing. Therefore, any mention of encompassing without an acronym relates to our version of encompassing, as presented next. The same applies to the versions of forecast encompassing in chapter 3 and simulation encompassing in chapter 5.

Our Version of Encompassing

There are two complementary components to encompassing as implemented in this book:

1. It focuses on the seminal interpretation of encompassing in sciences–specifically, does M_1, *as estimated under available data*, account for the findings of M_2? Therefore, it does not require any asymptotic assumptions. This is a critical difference from HMR and DGM, whose approaches rely upon asymptotic distributions that extend beyond the actual sample.

Examples of such auxiliary asymptotic assumptions include stationarity, unit roots, or cointegration. No such assumptions are required for our strictly finite sample simulation-based approach (obviously, it remains sound practice to rely upon inference techniques that have meaningful statistical properties).

2. It relies upon MSM estimation for two main reasons: (a) it only requires that the models under consideration be amenable to MC simulations; (b) as discussed further in chapter 4, it allows for critical flexibility in selecting those moments that are most likely to be affected by the empirical issue under scrutiny. A focus on such critical (or influential) moments considerably facilitates the interpretation of eventual encompassing successes and, foremost, failures.

For the ease of presentation and to avoid potential confusion, we discuss separately these two complementary components[3]:

1. Account for: Assume that we have estimated both M_1 and M_2, say, $\hat{M}_1 = M_1(\hat{\alpha})$ and $\hat{M}_2 = M_2(\hat{\delta})$. Encompassing amounts to testing whether $\hat{M}_1$ can account for $\hat{\delta}$. That is, whether $\hat{\delta}$ could have been generated by $\hat{M}_1$. All that is required to address this question is to use $\hat{M}_1$ to generate a set of S_2 simulated samples, such as $\{\tilde{y}_i\}, i: 1 \rightarrow S_2$. For each such sample, we then compute the corresponding estimate of δ. It is, then, a trivial matter to compute the corresponding sample mean and covariance matrix of $\hat{\delta}$ *under* $\hat{M}_1$, such as $\delta_1(\hat{\alpha})$ and $V_1(\hat{\alpha})$ respectively, from which we can compute either a global χ^2 encompassing test statistic for $\hat{\delta}$ or, more informatively, student-t encompassing test statistics for individual components of $\hat{\delta}$. A finding that $\hat{\delta}$ does not significantly differ from its simulated expectation $\delta_1(\hat{\alpha})$, given $\hat{M}_1$, is then interpreted as $\hat{M}_1$ encompasses $M_2(\hat{\delta})$. Foremost, by computing individual t-statistics, it is easy to identify those specific components of $\hat{\delta}$ that eventually are not encompassed by $M_1(\hat{\alpha})$, a critical component of further refinements of M_1.

   Actually, encompassing can be applied to any statistic of potential interest within M_2, not just parameters. Such flexibility could provide additional insights, especially in cases of failure to encompass.

   The intuition behind encompassing is that if $\hat{M}_1$ were a sufficiently good approximation of the unknown DGP (relative to the objectives of the analysis), one would expect that $\hat{\delta}$, which was estimated from data generated by the unknown DGP, might not be significantly different from its simulated mean under $\hat{M}_1$. The fact that this would not be the case asymptotically is largely irrelevant, as we are looking for policy conclusions derived from currently available data.

2. MSM: As discussed further in chapter 4, MSM starts with the selection of a set of sample moments (at least as many as parameters to be estimated), such as $\hat{m}(Y)$. This is a critical step, in that the MSM estimation of $\hat{\alpha}$ and $\hat{\delta}$, as well as the subsequent encompassing capabilities of $\hat{M}_1$, are largely driven by this initial selection of sample moments.[4] Therefore, one should always select moments that are thought to be most influential in the estimation of M_1. A GMM/MSM estimate for α and/or δ is obtained by minimizing a quadratic distance between $\hat{m}(Y)$ and its expected value under the model under consideration. The key difference is that GMM relies upon analytical expressions for these expected values, while MSM relies on MC simulations to compute them.

Specifically, for any tentative value of α, MSM relies upon auxiliary MC draws of the selected moments to compute their simulated expected mean vector and covariance matrix, conditional on $M_1(\alpha)$, from which one computes a quadratic objective function $f(\alpha)$ in the difference between $\hat{m}(Y)$ and its simulated sample mean, given α. An MSM estimate of α is obtained by minimization of that quadratic function. The same technique applies to compute an MSM estimate of δ under auxiliary draws from $M_2(\delta)$.

Our encompassing test procedure combines the "account for" principle with auxiliary MSM estimation of δ under simulated samples from $M_1(\hat{\alpha})$. It starts with the MSM estimation of both $M_1(\alpha)$ and $M_2(\delta)$.[5] Let $\hat{\alpha}$ and $\hat{\delta}$ denote the corresponding MSM estimates for those respective items. Then, to compute the finite sample mean and covariance matrix of $\hat{\delta}$ *conditional on* $M_1(\hat{\alpha})$, one relies upon nested loops of auxiliary MC simulations:

1. An outer loop of MC simulations from $M_1(\hat{\alpha})$ to produce a sequence of S_2 draws of the sample moments, such as $\hat{m}(\tilde{Y}_j)$ for $j : 1 \to S_2$;
2. For each $\hat{m}(\tilde{Y}_j)$, as many inner loops of S_1 auxiliary draws from $M_2(\delta)$ as needed to obtain the corresponding MSM estimate $\tilde{\delta}_j$, for $j = 1 \to S_2$.

The sequence of simulated MSM estimates $\{\tilde{\delta}_j\}$ is then used to compute the finite sample mean and covariance matrix of $\hat{\delta}$ conditional on $M_1(\hat{\alpha})$, and the corresponding encompassing global chi-squared or individual student-*t* statistics.

If this appears complicated at first reading, we shall see in chapter 5 that it is actually fairly simple to program, using a nested combination of an outer simulation module with an inner estimation module (as shown in tables 5.2 and 5.1, respectively).

What is the intuition behind our encompassing approach? It starts from the observation that the initial MSM estimates $\hat{\alpha}$ and $\hat{\delta}$ are obtained from sample moments produced by the unknown DGP. This being said, if $M_1(\hat{\alpha})$ turned out to be a good approximation to the unknown DGP, at least as far as accounting for $\hat{\delta}$ is concerned, one might expect moments simulated under $M_1(\hat{\alpha})$ to approximate the initial DGP sample moments. In such a case, the DGP-generated MSM estimate $\hat{\delta}$ might not be significantly different from its sample mean computed from a sequence of simulated moments drawn from $M_1(\hat{\alpha})$.

On the other hand, if $M_1(\hat{\alpha})$ were not a good approximation of the unknown DGP, one would expect that moments generated from $M_1(\hat{\alpha})$ would differ significantly from the initial DGP-generated moments, in which case $\hat{\delta}$ would also be significantly different from its $M_1(\hat{\alpha})$-simulated mean, at least for some of its components.

An important issue is the origin of M_2. The presumption is that M_1 was constructed in a thoughtful and deliberate manner. M_2 could be an alternative model from another researcher that can be estimated using the data that produced the M_1 estimates. But there is an important and readily accessible alternative construction of M_2. Presumably, M_1 was constructed to measure the impact of some potential conduct by economic actors. Then M_2 can be created by taking the M_1 model and restricting the impact of the conduct to be zero. For example, M_1 might be a model of labor market compensation that accounts for potential discrimination by employers, while M_2 is the same model but with no potential discrimination by employers. Loosely put, M_2 is nested within M_1. Can M_1 encompass M_2?

While an initial reaction to that question might be that (obviously) a nesting model can account for a nested model, the actual answer critically depends on the context and, in particular, on an unambiguous, generic definition of nesting[6] that is not model specific.

There are indeed a few special situations where nesting does imply encompassing. In particular, under a null hypothesis that $M_1(\alpha)$ is the DGP, it would obviously encompass any $M_2(\delta)$ statistics obtained from the same data, not only those nested within $M_1(\alpha)$. But, at the risk of being redundant, we know that M_1 will never be the DGP for any serious empirical application, which is precisely why we do not test whether $M_1(\hat{\alpha})$ is the DGP, only whether it can account for $\hat{\delta}$.

Another special case is that when $M_1(\alpha)$ and $M_2(\delta)$ are both unrestricted linear models. In such a case, as discussed further in section 2.4.4, if M_2 is nested within M_1 in the sense that $\hat{\delta} \equiv h(\hat{\alpha})$, then encompassing follows.

Except for these special cases, it is generally not true that nesting implies encompassing, as highlighted by example 2.9.2 and, foremost, by the Idaho Department of Lands (IDL) timber auctions application in chapter 6.

Suppose that M_1 cannot account for an alternative model M_2. Even though considerable thoughtfulness and deliberation went into the construction of M_1, how could one legitimately use M_1 to make policy recommendations or construct counterfactuals? In this case, there clearly is some deficiency of M_1 as an approximation of the unknown DGP.

But this is a constructive outcome, not a destructive one. If M_1 cannot account for an alternative model M_2, then we can examine the specific parameters where encompassing failed and see how to potentially improve M_1. Improvements of M_1, guided by the inability to encompass M_2, can lead to a revised M_1, which then does encompass M_2. We argue that this revised M_1 provides a much sounder foundation for policy recommendations and counterfactuals than does the original M_1.

So far, this entire discussion has been about the parameters of M_2. But encompassing is not limited to those parameters. Any statistic that can be produced by M_2 can be the focus of an encompassing test. One such statistic is forecast errors. Unlike earlier literature on forecast encompassing, which focused on combinations of forecasts from M_1 and M_2, our version of forecast encompassing is a straightforward application of encompassing. We develop this concept in chapter 3.

We present a serious empirical application in chapter 6. Anyone can see from the data appendix that a great deal of time and care were taken in understanding the data. Similar care is reflected in the main text regarding an understanding of the institutional features of the market. Our focus there is on IDL timber auctions. We develop a model of potential bidder collusion at these auctions. Let us call that model M_1^*. By setting the parameters associated with collusion to zero in M_1^* we get a noncollusive model, which we call M_2. Finally, a model of bidder collusion was developed in the literature over two decades ago, different from M_1^*, which we call M_1. Each of these models was estimated using MSM, and encompassing was applied to both M_1 and M_2 under M_1^*, as well as to M_1^* under M_1.

What did we find? M_1^* encompasses M_1. However, M_1 also encompasses M_1^*! Yes, mutual encompassing can occur. Why is that? Simply put, each of the collusive models may be capturing different aspects of the DGP, and nevertheless, each can account for the other under a finite sample (e.g., as the result of significant correlation between the respective model specific omitted variables).

We also find that M_1^* encompasses M_2 but M_1 does not encompass M_2. What does that mean in terms of the usefulness of the two collusive models? M_1^* should be used for policy recommendations since it encompasses both M_1 and

M_2. M_1^* implies a loss of $81 million for the state of Idaho from bidder collusion over the time period that we investigated.

There is a large body of historical literature on this topic, which is discussed in subsequent chapters. Chapter 2 concerns the central issue of the book, encompassing. chapter 3 addresses forecast encompassing. Chapters 4 and 5 concern simulation methods and their implementation with regard to encompassing. Chapter 6 contains the timber auction application. Concluding comments can be found in chapter 7.

2

Encompassing

Chapter 2 is organized as follows. The generic concept of encompassing is introduced in section 2.1. Section 2.2 presents an extensive review of the encompassing literature, followed by a discussion in section 2.3. The DGM and HMR versions of encompassing are reviewed in section 2.4. Section 2.5 presents our version of encompassing. Section 2.6 offers a summary of the differences among the three versions of encompassing. Feasibility and exogeneity are discussed in sections 2.7 and 2.8, respectively. A number of examples are presented in section 2.9, and section 2.10 briefly discusses eventual generalizations. Technical details are provided in appendices 2A and 2B.

2.1 The Concept of Encompassing

The notion that a new model ought to account for, hereafter encompass, the findings (successes as well as failures) from previous models is fundamental to sciences and characterizes progressive research strategies. For example, Popper (1963) argues that "tentative theories" should be subjected to rigorous attempts at falsification: "If it is not falsifiable, it is not science." This process of error elimination performs a function for science similar to natural selection in biological evolution. Lakatos (1978) adopts a more nuanced approach, which still relies upon falsifiability but interprets it in the context of "research programs" (i.e., sequences of theories). Such a program is deemed to constitute good science if it is both theoretically and empirically progressive.

A striking illustration of such progress can be found in the spectacular advances in physics and cosmology over the last 100 years with such landmarks as general relativity, the Big Bang, galaxies, supernovas, expanding universe, black holes, inflation, cosmic microwave background, and currently the elusive search for dark matter and dark energy. More recently, "based in part on what the (James Webb Space) telescope has revealed, it's beginning to look as if we may need to rethink key features of the origin and development of the universe" (Frank and Gleiser, 2023, section SR, p. 8).

In economics, we don't have access to such complex and expensive research instruments. Foremost, we are dealing with societal behavior, for which we can't expect convergence toward some grand unified theory. Nevertheless, we strongly believe that encompassing ought to be a fundamental component of progressive research in economics. A formal, operational definition of simulation encompassing will be provided in chapter 5.

2.2 Literature Review

To structure our presentation of the current leading implementations of encompassing, our literature review is divided into five sections: (1) early related concepts; (2) the HMR approach; (3) the DGM approach; (4) later contributions; and (5) Bayesian encompassing.

2.2.1 Early Related Concepts

Initially, econometric methodology, such as described in Theil (1957, 1961), focused on the problem of choosing among alternative models, assuming that one of the choices under consideration should be the true model (referred to as the DGP in our subsequent analysis). Therefore, any selection criterion (e.g., tests based on residual variances) should select the true model at least as often as the alternatives. Relatedly, classical test procedures such as the F-test could be applied only to nested hypotheses (loosely, hypotheses that are members of the same family). A formal definition of nesting will be provided in section 2.4.4, as the concept of nested versus non nested models plays a critical role in the formal definitions of encompassing to be introduced later in this chapter.

Cox (1961, 1962) proposed an original theory for testing "separate families of hypotheses" and proposed a statistic, now referred to as "Cox's test statistic," based upon the loglikelihood difference between the competing hypotheses. That statistic relied upon technical derivations that, as will be discussed, would later be expanded into formal definitions of encompassing.

Pesaran (1974, 154) derived a procedure for testing non nested regression models based on Cox's theory. He also offered comments that will prove highly relevant in the context of the present book: "Furthermore, the requirement that one of the models under consideration should be the 'true model' is very unlikely to be satisfied in practice. Consequently, it seems more appropriate to treat the problem of choosing alternative models as a hypothesis testing problem rather than an arbitrary definition of what the 'true model' should be."

Pesaran and Deaton (1978, 678) generalized Pesaran's approach to non nested nonlinear regression models. They also commented: "In econometrics, we never have a maintained hypothesis which we believe with certainty; we must always use the models we possess to organize the evidence in different ways and to ask whether the patterns which results are consistent with the views we currently hold." Another quote, which contains the essence of later concepts of encompassing, is: "An hypothesis, which one would not wish to consider seriously in its own right, can be a perfectly effective tool for disproving an alternative, even if that alternative may in some respects seem much more promising."

Davidson, Hendry, Srba and Yeo (1978, 661) cite a "plethora of substantially different quarterly regression equations" relative to the relationship between consumers' expenditure and disposable income in the UK. The authors discuss at length a concept of "constructive" research strategy, whereby "any model which fails to account for the 'gestalt' of results which are obtained from the dataset cannot constitute the actual data generation process. Consequently, a further minimal requirement when modelling from a common dataset is that the chosen model should explain both the *results* obtained by other researchers and *why* their research methods led to their published conclusions." They specifically refer to this requirement as "encompassing previous findings," (662), which, to the best of our knowledge, was the first explicit mention of encompassing in a major empirical study.

As the three leading models under consideration were conditioned by different hypotheses, the authors' initial step consisted of reframing them as nested versions of a more general model and then relying upon standard nested tests. In the process, they were able to explain key differences among the initial models.

Along similar lines, Hendry and Ericsson (1991) develop "constant, data coherent," narrow money demand equations for the US and UK. Next, they use these equations to investigate a variety of issues associated with earlier models, such as the "missing money" puzzle, the velocity decline, and the narrow money "recent explosion." Again, the authors' approach is very much in the spirit of the formal definitions of encompassing presented here.

The papers we review next are closer to the main objective of our book, which is that of verifying whether one's preferred parametric model $M_1(\alpha)$ can account for (i.e., encompass) results derived under an alternative (e.g., counterfactual) parametric model $M_2(\delta)$.

2.2.2 Hendry, Mizon and Richard (HMR)

Numerous discussions among the three co-authors lead to a formal definition of "parametric encompassing," together with applications. See Hendry and Richard (1982), Mizon (1984), Mizon and Richard (1986), and Hendry and Richard (1989). Technical details are omitted in this literature review; they will be addressed in section 2.4, where we introduce the relevant notation and definitions. In a nutshell, parametric encompassing amounts to testing whether the encompassing difference between parameter estimates of $M_2(\delta)$ and their probability limits under $M_1(\alpha)$ converges to zero, conditionally on $M_1(\alpha)$.

In Hendry and Richard (1982, definition 11) "Cox-encompassing" is presented as one key component of an "integrated progressive research strategy." It is illustrated by an analysis of the choice of regressors problem in the context of linear dynamic models.

Mizon (1984) and Mizon and Richard (1986, definition 3) use the same definition, relabeled as complete parametric encompassing (CPE). The authors also consider generalizations, whereby the statistics to be encompassed depend upon the data, in addition to the parameters of M_2. Both Wald encompassing tests (WET) and score encompassing tests (SET) are defined. An extensive application to the linear choice of regressors problem leads to encompassing reinterpretations of commonly used test statistics such as the F-test, the Hausman (1978) specification test, the Davidson and MacKinnon (1981) J-test, and the Godfrey (1983) T_X statistic. The authors also discuss an important concept of "implicit null hypotheses," which is defined as the subset of models for which a given test has zero asymptotic power. They show that the aforementioned test statistics have different implicit null hypotheses unless one makes the empirically unreasonable assumption that the DGP belongs to $\{M_1, M_2\}$.

Hendry and Richard (1989) provide a survey of the concept of parametric encompassing, together with important additional extensions. Foremost, they explicitly refer to an underlying unknown DGP and draw a distinction between the earlier "sampling" definition of parametric encompassing (definition 1) and an asymptotic concept of "population encompassing" (definition 2). As we shall see, that distinction is a critical component of the DGM definition of encompassing. Nevertheless, the focus of the paper remains parametric encompassing and its role as an "integrated concept for modelling," together with examples.

The authors also introduce a concept of "parsimonious encompassing," whereby model M_2 encompasses a larger model M_1 within which it is nested, a concept that will play a central role in "model reduction," as discussed in section 2.4.4.

Last but not least, and directly related to the objective of our book, the authors describe how to rely upon MC simulations of M_1 to construct a finite sample distribution for the parametric encompassing test statistics.

2.2.3 Dhaene, Gourieroux and Monfort (DGM)

While, as mentioned previously, Hendry and Richard (1989) alluded to the role of an underlying DGP, a pioneering, formal, loglikelihood-based treatment of encompassing is offered by Gouriéroux and Monfort (1995), taking explicitly into account the fact that the true distribution does not necessarily belong to one of the competing models. Their analysis is fairly technical and relies upon the fundamental concept of Kullback-Leibler information criterion (KLIC) as a loglikelihood-based distance measure between models. The authors introduce a number of KLIC-related concepts, such as pseudo-true values, binding functions, and image and reflecting sets, setting the scene for a formal definition of encompassing. Operational approximations of these concepts, together with a graphical illustration will be presented in section 2.4.

This formal framework enables the authors to clarify two critical issues in their introduction:

1. "For instance, a model including another one does not necessarily encompass this model, or if a model encompasses another model it does not necessarily encompass a submodel of this model." We discuss this issue further in section 2.4.4.
2. "Tests of the encompassing conditions should be performed without assuming that the true probability distribution function (p.d.f.) necessarily belongs to one of the competing models." As discussed in chapter 1, this is actually the key motivation for the concept of encompassing introduced in section 2.5.

The authors demonstrate that the Cox approach is not appropriate for testing encompassing. They analyze a number of alternatives: WET, SET, and a simpler generalized encompassing test (GET). Noting that the relevant "binding functions" are often unknown (e.g., because the distribution of the exogenous variables is unknown), the authors propose replacing them by finite sample simulated versions thereof and define accordingly simulated WET and GET statistics.

While their approach is fundamental to set the encompassing principle on a sound theoretical basis, it relies upon complex loglikelihood-based derivations that are clearly beyond the reach of practitioners and serious empirical applications such as that presented in chapter 6.

Dhaene (1997) provides a significantly more abstract and exhaustive treatment of encompassing in terms of σ-finite measure spaces and related families of distributions. As was the case with Gouriéroux and Monfort (1995), Dhaene's approach relies on KLIC. Dhaene (1997) chapter 2 figures 1 and 2 illustrate some of the key concepts. The theoretical advantage of Dhaene's formal approach is that of providing a rigorous and unambiguous analysis of the properties of the encompassing relation (section 2.4), such as non transitivity (property 4.17) and mutual encompassing (property 4.14). Foremost, Dhaene (1997, page 45) asserts that: "It is a fundamental property of the DGP that the performance of any model, no matter how badly misspecified, is completely determined by the DGP, whatever the definition of "performance" may be. By this, we mean that one can, at least in principle, derive from the DGP the distribution of any estimator, statistic, test outcome, etc. . . . which arises in the course of empirical model building. Also, the DGP determines the pseudo-true values associated with the models whenever they exist."

Tests of unambiguously defined hypotheses are presented in Dhaene's chapter 3 (p. 55), where he argues that "the theory of encompassing provides a unified framework for interpreting" a large variety of existing approaches for testing hypotheses that can be expressed by means of parametric families. In chapter 4, Dhaene presents a comprehensive analysis of encompassing tests for the linear model, together with eventual asymptotic equivalences.

Dhaene's conclusion provides a fundamental validation of the encompassing approach: "Generally speaking, models are intended to mimic relevant aspects of the true process generating the data. Quite fundamentally, from the true process it is always possible to predict the results obtained from a given model $\mathcal{G}$, relative to the uncertainty involved. Hence, the finding that another model $\mathcal{F}$ can mimic this fundamental feature of the true process is evidence in favour of $\mathcal{F}$, whereas the failure of $\mathcal{F}$ to mimic this feature reveals shortcomings of $\mathcal{F}$ as an approximation to the true process."

2.2.4 Later Contributions

Dhaene, Gouriéroux and Scaillet (1998) propose (among other tests) an indirect, simulation-based version of encompassing in the context of recursive dynamic models. Such models often have analytically intractable loglikelihood functions, so the "binding functions" (defined in section 2.4) required for encompassing may not exist in closed form. However, they can be simulated for any tentative values of the parameters.

Therefore, indirect estimation based on simulations and an auxiliary criterion function can be used to replace direct estimation. For example, see Smith (1993), Gouriéroux and Monfort (1993), and Gallant and Tauchen (1996). As was the case in section 2.2.3, the authors explicitly account for the role of the DGP, which leads them to distinguish between "well-specified and misspecified models."

The paper is quite technical, but it presents an important analogy with our own implementation of MSM and simulation encompassing, as discussed in chapters 4 and 5. Specifically, the parameters of the auxiliary models serve as target moments and simulation is used to evaluate their expected values as a function of the parameters of the model under consideration. Minimization of a quadratic distance between the target moments and their simulated expected values produces the indirect estimates that are then used to compute a variety of test statistics, including indirect encompassing tests.

Wooldridge (1990, 331) proposes a class of conditional mean encompassing (CME) tests "that are more operational than the Complete Parametric Encompassing (CPE) tests proposed by Mizon and Richard (1986)." These are designed to detect misspecification of the conditional expectations for cross-sections or time-series models and do not require solving for pseudo-true values for the parameters of the alternative model. The author considers two models (null H_0 and alternative H_1), which differ by the functional form of their expectations conditional on a set of predetermined variables. In contrast with DGM, there is no reference to an underlying DGP that might differ from the models under consideration.

The CME test statistic is based on the covariance between the gradient of the alternative H_1 regression function and the residuals fitted under H_0. It amounts to looking for departures from H_0 in the direction of H_1. It follows that the CME test is a Newey-Tauchen-White conditional moment test using that gradient as the misspecification indicator. See Newey (1985), Tauchen (1985), and White (1987) for further details and references.

Lu, Mizon and Monfardini (2008) rely upon simulations to compute the WET and Cox test statistics. The baseline implementation is the same as that briefly outlined by Hendry and Richard (1989, section 12.5), but its validation is based on rigorous asymptotic derivations, treating M_1 "as being the DGP." This assumption is similar to that used in the HMR approach (see section 2.2.2). It is a critical assumption that we shall relax in the simulation encompassing approach presented in chapter 5.

The authors apply their simulation procedure to the Cox statistic for testing linear versus loglinear models, assuming that the linear model is the DGP. They conduct an extensive simulation experiment. In particular, they compare statistics for which only the numerator of the statistic is simulated to those where both the numerator and denominator are simulated. A remarkable result is that the latter systematically outperform the former. This is good news for the approach proposed in this book, which is entirely simulation-based.

Campos, Ericsson and Hendry (2005) provide a detailed overview of general-to-specific modeling. In their section 4.7, the authors discuss several of the papers that we have reviewed here.

Hendry, Marcellino and Mizon (2008) edited a special issue on encompassing, in which they introduce the principle of encompassing and present a simple example. The contributors present a broad overview of many of the issues discussed here.

Hendry and Doornik (2014) present an in-depth discussion of the principle of dynamic model selection, of which parsimonious encompassing is a key component for model "reduction." Specifically, the authors advocate starting from an overparameterized linear general unrestricted model (GUM) meant to closely approximate an underlying local DGP. A progressive research strategy then consists of implementing successive reductions of the GUM by recursive application of a parsimonious encompassing F-test, noting that Govaerts, Hendry and Richard (1994) have demonstrated the advantage of that test against alternatives. The outcome of that exercise is a reduced model that parsimoniously encompasses the initial GUM. This parsimonious encompassing process is incorporated in the Autometrics software, as described in Doornik (2009) and Hendry and Doornik (2014). Nesting and parsimonious or mutual encompassing are discussed futher in section 2.4.4.

2.2.5 Bayesian Encompassing

In the 1990s, several papers developed a Bayesian concept of encompassing. See, for example, Florens (1990); Florens and Mouchart (1989), which includes an extensive list of references; Florens and Mouchart (1993); and Florens, Hendry and Richard (1996). We note that these papers preceded the DGM contributions reviewed in section 2.2.3. Therefore, except for occasional references to an underlying DGP, one is essentially discussing a transition between posterior densities associated with a pair of models, M_1 and M_2. Generally, there is asymmetry between the two models, in that the parameters of interest are functions of the parameters of M_1 only. The Bayesian extension of HMR is conceptually straightforward.

Estimators are replaced by posterior densities and Bayesian encompassing becomes the question of whether the posterior density of the parameters of M_2 obtains from that of the parameters of M_1 by means of a transition density that is independent of the sample and which is the Bayesian counterpart of the classical concept of "binding function," defined in section 2.4.

While such a formulation has limited empirical applicability, it offers important conceptual clarifications. For example, by permuting parameters and statistics, one obtains a version of the concept of sufficiency among statistics, as introduced by Blackwell (1951, 1953). Such "duality" leads to interpreting encompassing as a notion of sufficiency among "inference procedures" (i.e., posterior densities). Relatedly, exactly as LeCam (1964) relies upon a notion of deficiency to measure a lack of sufficiency, one can define a concept of "specificity" that aims at measuring a lack of exact encompassing.

Last but not least, as it would typically be the case that M_1 and M_2 would have different owners, the issue of eventual incompatibility between the respective prior densities naturally arises. Accordingly, Florens, Hendry and Richard (1996) introduce a concept of "coherent" encompassing, whereby a common transition density applies to prior as well as posterior densities. The authors apply the various encompassing concepts to the conventional "choice of regressors" problem, where all derivations under "natural conjugate priors" are analytical.

This being said, while "informal priors" are inherent to any empirical application, formal application of these Bayesian encompassing concepts to serious empirical applications, such as that analyzed in chapter 6, is all but unfeasible.

2.3 Discussion

There are several key issues that emerge from our review of the encompassing literature in sections 2.2.2 to 2.2.4:

1. It is fundamentally loglikelihood-based, which essentially prevents its application to substantive empirical issues, for which a loglikelihood function and its derivatives will generally not be operational. Therefore, it is not surprising that empirical applications of encompassing have largely been limited to linear dynamic models, for which conventional F-test statistics can be reinterpreted as tests for parsimonious encompassing (Hendry and Doornik, 2014).

   The approach that we propose here will apply to any consistent estimator, including MSM. When combined with MC simulations, it will require no complex analytical derivations.

2. A fundamental difference between HMR and DGM lies in the role attributed to the unknown DGP (say $M_0(\theta)$). Under HMR, there are occasional references to an unknown DGP, such as in the definition of "population encompassing" (Hendry and Richard, 1989, definition 2 and figure 12.1), or that of "implicit null hypotheses" (Mizon and Richard, 1986, section 4). Fundamentally, however, the distribution of the encompassing statistic is derived under the model M_1 under scrutiny. As we shall illustrate in this discussion, this has important implications for the interpretation of a positive outcome.

   In sharp contrast, under DGM, the very definition of encompassing involves the unknown DGP (Gouriéroux and Monfort, 1995, section 2.4);

and (Dhaene, 1997, section 4.3). While the DGM approach relies on a more rigorous statistical analysis of encompassing than the HMR approach, it also significantly complicates the derivation of the properties of encompassing test statistics.

3. Encompassing has often been reinterpreted within a conventional testing framework (maintained, null, and alternative). In particular, it has led to encompassing reinterpretations of several standard tests for non nested hypotheses such as the choice of regressors problem (see, e.g., Mizon and Richard, 1986, section 3). In such a case, it becomes an issue of choosing between two alternative models (say, M_1 and M_2) instead of the more fundamental encompassing concept, which is that of verifying whether one's preferred model M_1 can account for results obtained under M_2, thereby mimicking a fundamental property of the unknown DGP M_0.

   We don't think that this testing framework would be of interest in most policy-relevant applications. Specifically, M_1 would typically represent one's preferred model, obtained after months of careful investigation of the issues under consideration, extensive data collection efforts, complex programming, and successive refinements of the initial model. Obviously, encompassing an alternative model M_2 (whether a restricted version of M_1 or an earlier model) remains essential as to whether to validate M_1 as an approximation of the unknown DGP, or identify aspects of M_2, which M_1 cannot account for. Either way, it would be unrealistic to consider replacing M_1 with M_2 in view of the very large M_1 sunk costs. Instead, failure to encompass should lead to further refinements of M_1, with the objective of addressing specific encompassing failures, if it is at all possible under data limitations.

Relatedly, it is not necessary that M_2 be a credible alternative to M_1. In many cases, M_2 deficiencies might have been the very reasons for developing a new model M_1. Nevertheless, it remains the case that in order to approximate the unknown DGP, M_1 ought to encompass M_2.

2.4 DGM and HMR Encompassing

To present the operational encompassing approach proposed in this book and to compare it to the HMR and DGM approaches reviewed here, we first need to introduce notations and definitions. Foremost, the DGM key concepts of "pseudo-true values" and "binding functions," which rely upon the log-likelihood-based concept of Kullback-Leibler distance (Kullback and Leibler, 1951), are replaced by corresponding definitions in terms of probability limits (hereafter plims') that apply to any consistent estimator under the relevant models.

2.4.1 Notations and Definitions

- $M_0(\theta)$: the unknown DGP (could be non-parametric)
- $\mathcal{M} = \{M_0(\theta); \theta \in \Theta\}$
- $M_1(\alpha), \alpha \in A \subseteq R^k$: one's preferred model
- $\mathcal{M}_1 = \{M_1(\alpha); \alpha \in A\}$; it will generally be the case that $M_0(\theta) \notin \mathcal{M}_1$
- $M_2(\delta)$, $\delta \in D \subseteq R^l$: a model to be potentially encompassed
- $\mathcal{M}_2 = \{M_2(\delta); \delta \in D\}$
- N: sample size
- $\hat{\alpha}_N$ and $\hat{\delta}_N$ denote the following consistent estimators:

$$\operatorname*{plim}_{M_1(\alpha)} \hat{\alpha}_N = \alpha; \qquad \operatorname*{plim}_{M_2(\delta)} \hat{\delta}_N = \delta \tag{2.1}$$

The following DGM loglikelihood-based definitions are reformulated in terms of plims and are illustrated in figure 2.2.

- Pseudo-true values:

$$\alpha_0(\theta) = \operatorname*{plim}_{M_0(\theta)} \hat{\alpha}_N; \qquad \delta_0(\theta) = \operatorname*{plim}_{M_0(\theta)} \hat{\delta}_N. \tag{2.2}$$

- Binding functions:

$$\delta_1(\alpha) = \operatorname*{plim}_{M_1(\alpha)} \hat{\delta}_N; \qquad \alpha_2(\delta) = \operatorname*{plim}_{M_2(\delta)} \hat{\alpha}_N. \tag{2.3}$$

2.4.2 DGM Encompassing

A population definition of encompassing can be found in Gouriéroux and Monfort (1995, equation (4.1)); see also Dhaene (1997, definition 3.1):

$$H_0^{DGM} : \phi_0(\theta) = \delta_0(\theta) - \delta_1(\alpha_0(\theta)) = 0. \tag{2.4}$$

Tests of encompassing are based upon the encompassing difference defined as:

$$\hat{\phi}_N = \hat{\delta}_N - \delta_1(\hat{\alpha}_N). \tag{2.5}$$

The main problem is that of deriving the distribution of $\hat{\phi}_N$ under H_0^{DGM}. The authors demonstrate that

$$\sqrt{N}\hat{\phi}_N \xrightarrow[H_0^{DGM}]{} N(0, \Omega_0), \tag{2.6}$$

where Ω_0 has a complicated analytical loglikelihood-based expression and could be singular. The corresponding WET statistic is given by

$$\xi_N^W = N\hat{\phi}_N' \hat{\Omega}_0^+ \hat{\phi}_N \xrightarrow[H_0^{DGM}]{} \chi^2(d), \tag{2.7}$$

where $\hat{\Omega}_0^+$ denotes a generalized inverse of an estimate $\hat{\Omega}_0$ of Ω_0 with rank d.

A problem with this approach, beyond its inherent complexity, is that the binding function δ_1 depends on the unknown distribution of the exogenous variables. The authors then introduce a simulated WET statistic that replaces the unknown $\delta_1(\alpha)$ by a simulated finite sample counterpart.

It is fair to say that while the DGM approach represents the statistically most rigorous approach to encompassing, it is unfeasible for the serious empirical application we have in mind.

2.4.3 HMR Encompassing

As discussed in Mizon and Richard (1986), among other sources, the HMR approach is based upon the asymptotic distribution of the encompassing difference (or "encompassing contrast") $\sqrt{N}\hat{\phi}_N$ under $M_1(\alpha)$, instead of the unknown DGP $M_0(\theta)$:

$$\sqrt{N}\hat{\phi}_N \xrightarrow[M_1(\alpha)]{} N(0, V_\alpha(\sqrt{N}\hat{\phi}_N)), \text{ where} \tag{2.8}$$

$$V_\alpha(\sqrt{N}\hat{\phi}_N) = V_\alpha(\sqrt{N}\hat{\delta}_N) - DV_\alpha(\sqrt{N}\hat{\alpha}_N)D' \tag{2.9}$$

$$D = \frac{\partial(\delta_1(\alpha))}{\partial \alpha'}. \tag{2.10}$$

For instance, see Cox (1962), Gouriéroux and Monfort (1993), and Domowitz and White (1982). The corresponding WET statistic is given by

$$\eta_N^W = N\hat{\phi}_N' V_\alpha^+(\sqrt{N}\hat{\phi}_N)\hat{\phi}_N, \tag{2.11}$$

where V_α^+ denotes a generalized inverse of V_α. There are two problems with the asymptotic formulas (2.8) to (2.11):

1. We have access to only a finite sample of size N (Therefore, we delete the fixed subscript N in subsequent formulas).
2. Relatedly, we don't know α and have only an estimate $\hat{\alpha}$ thereof.

Therefore, finite sample estimates of the asymptotic moments $\delta_1(\alpha)$ and $V_\alpha(\hat{\phi})$ in equations (2.8) to (2.10) obtain by replacing α by $\hat{\alpha}$, such as

$$d_1(\hat{\alpha}) = \mathbb{E}(\hat{\delta}|M_1(\alpha))|_{\alpha=\hat{\alpha}}, \qquad \hat{\phi} = \hat{\delta} - d_1(\hat{\alpha}) \tag{2.12}$$

$$V_1(\hat{\alpha}) = \text{Var}(\hat{\phi}|M_1(\alpha))|_{\alpha=\hat{\alpha}}. \tag{2.13}$$

The corresponding (finite sample) HMR-WET statistic is then given by

$$\hat{\eta}_W^{HMR} = \hat{\phi}' V_1^+(\hat{\alpha})\hat{\phi}. \tag{2.14}$$

The HMR approach calls for several comments:

1. Foremost, it is apparent from equations (2.8) and (2.14) that HMR amounts to testing the following implicit null hypothesis:

$$H_0^{HMR} : \underset{M_1(\alpha)}{\text{plim}}\, \hat{\phi}_N = 0. \tag{2.15}$$

   Note that, as discussed in chapter 1, it makes no sense to interpret $M_1(\alpha)$ as a tentative, or even partial DGP. Foremost, economic reality is inherently far more complex than any model thereof. Moreover, key variables that affect the DGP are not observable and others are conditioned upon. This is why the assumption H_0^{HMR} in equation (2.15) is formulated in terms of the limiting behavior of $\hat{\phi}_N$ under $M_1(\alpha)$, not in terms of an explicit asymptotic link between $M_1(\alpha)$ and the unknown DGP. Obviously, a finding that $\hat{\phi}$ is not significantly different from zero can be interpreted as an indication that $\hat{M}_1$ mimics the underlying DGP, insofar as accounting for $\hat{M}_2$.
2. The notation in equation (2.13) can be misleading. What is at stake is the *joint* distribution of $(\hat{\alpha}, \hat{\delta})$, from which that of $\hat{\phi}$ obtains, under samples drawn from $\hat{M}_1 = M_1(\hat{\alpha})$ as estimated. Specifically, to compute $V_1(\hat{\alpha})$ by MC simulation, we need to draw a sequence of S_2 auxiliary samples from $\hat{M}_1$ and to compute the corresponding sequence of $(\hat{\alpha}, \hat{\delta}, \hat{\phi})$ estimates from which $V_1(\hat{\alpha})$ obtains. This critical HMR feature will be illustrated in examples 2.9.1 and 2.9.2 and further clarified in chapter 5, where we discuss simulation encompassing.
3. In serious empirical applications, it would be unrealistic to expect $M_0(\theta)$– or any valid reduction thereof–to be in $\mathcal{M}_1$. In such a case, the finite sample version of equations (2.4) and (2.5) would be

$$\mathbb{E}(\hat{\phi}|M_0(\theta)) = \phi_0(\theta) \neq 0. \tag{2.16}$$

   Figures 2.1 and 2.2 illustrate the difference between the plims of the encompassing difference $\hat{\phi} = \hat{\delta} - \delta_1(\hat{\alpha})$ under HMR and DGM. Let $\mathcal{M}_1 = \{M_1(\alpha), \alpha \in A\}$ and $\mathcal{M}_2 = \{M_2(\delta), \delta \in D\}$. The subscript N inherent in plim calculations is omitted for notational convenience. KLIC distances are represented by orthogonal projections (as dotted lines on both figures) on the relevant parameter spaces: In both cases, we assume that $\hat{\alpha} \in A \backslash D$. It follows that $\delta_1(\hat{\alpha})$ is the projection of $\hat{\alpha}$ on D.

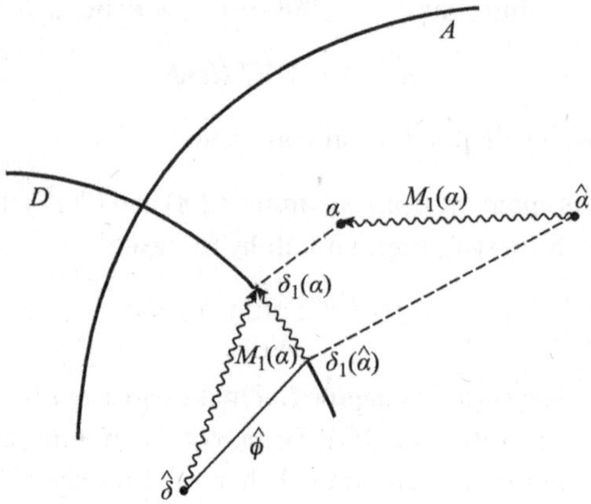

Figure 2.1
HMR, when $\alpha \in A$.

Figure 2.1 illustrates convergence under HMR when there exists $\alpha \in A$, such that $\hat{\alpha}$, as estimated from data produced by the unknown DGP, would actually converge to $\alpha \in A$. Convergence under H_0^{HMR} is represented by the $M_1(\alpha)$ wiggled lines with

$$\alpha = \operatorname*{plim}_{M_1(\alpha)} \hat{\alpha}, \qquad \text{and } \delta_1(\alpha) = \operatorname*{plim}_{M_1(\alpha)} \hat{\delta}, \tag{2.17}$$

both in A. Therefore, under H_0^{HMR}, we have

$$\operatorname*{plim}_{M_1(\alpha)} \hat{\phi} = \operatorname*{plim}_{M_1(\alpha)} \hat{\delta} - \operatorname*{plim}_{M_1(\alpha)} \delta_1(\hat{\alpha}) = \delta_1(\alpha) - \delta_1(\alpha) = 0. \tag{2.18}$$

Figure 2.2 illustrates DGM convergence when the unknown DGP $M_0(\theta) \notin \mathcal{M}_1$ (i.e., $\theta \notin A$). Convergence under $M_0(\theta)$ is represented by the $M_0(\theta)$ wiggled lines, and we have

$$\alpha(\theta) = \operatorname*{plim}_{M_0(\theta)} \hat{\alpha}, \qquad \delta(\theta) = \operatorname*{plim}_{M_0(\theta)} \hat{\delta}, \qquad \delta_1(\alpha(\theta)) = \operatorname*{plim}_{M_0(\theta)} \delta_1(\hat{\alpha}), \tag{2.19}$$

where $\delta_1(\alpha(\theta))$ is the KLIC projection of $\alpha(\theta)$ on D. It follows that under DGM and with $\theta \notin \mathcal{M}_1$, we have

$$\operatorname*{plim}_{M_0(\theta)} \hat{\phi} = \operatorname*{plim}_{M_0(\theta)} \hat{\delta} - \operatorname*{plim}_{M_0(\theta)} \delta_1(\hat{\alpha}) = \delta(\theta) - \delta_1(\alpha(\theta)) \neq 0. \tag{2.20}$$

Figure 2.2 also heuristically indicates that if the KLIC distance between θ and $\alpha(\theta)$ decreased, so would the distance between $\delta(\theta)$ and $\delta_1(\alpha(\theta))$. Therefore, it is appropriate to interpret a finding that $\hat{\phi}$ is not significantly different from zero as "evidence in favor of" $M_1(\alpha)$ (Dhaene, 1997).

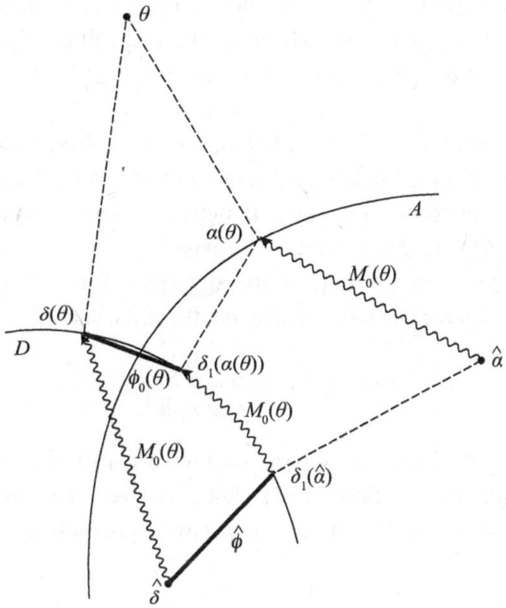

Figure 2.2
DGM, when $\theta \notin A$.

4. An additional problem arises when HMR is interpreted within a classical testing framework in which case, as pointed out by Mizon and Richard (1986, section 4.1) and foremost by DGM, the implication of rejecting H_0^{HMR} critically depends on the specific testing framework (null, alternative, and maintained hypotheses). For example, within a formal model choice framework, where the maintained hypothesis is $\{M_1, M_2\}$, rejection of H_0^{HMR} would imply selecting M_2, which is clearly an unacceptable outcome in any serious empirical application.

   Alternatively, if we refer back to the fundamental motivation of encompassing as a key component of a progressive research strategy, as discussed in section 2.1, rejection of H_0^{HMR} ought to be interpreted as a finding that there are aspects of $M_2(\hat{\delta})$ that $M_1(\hat{\alpha})$ cannot account for and a call for further improvement of $M_1(\hat{\alpha})$ in the direction of $M_2(\hat{\delta})$.

Actually, while much of the emphasis in HMR is set on providing a unifying, encompassing interpretation for a number of existing test statistics for nested as well as non nested hypotheses, the authors are well aware of the foundational motivation of encompassing, whereby rejection serves to provide guidelines for further improvements of one's current model $M_1(\alpha)$, if at all possible.

"Either M_1 is therefore *rejected* or, more constructively, such evidence may contribute toward improving M_1 whenever these specific features are relevant to the objectives of the proprietor of M_1" (Hendry and Richard, 1989, section 12.3).

Accordingly, (Mizon and Richard, 1986, section 4, 408) recommend that, in case of rejection of the CPE test associated with the WET statistic in equation (2.14), one could rely on incomplete parametric encompassing tests "to identify those aspects of M_2 that M_1 cannot encompass."

Along these lines, we can replace the aggregate WET statistic in equation (2.14) by t-statistics for the individual $\hat{\phi}$ coefficients, such as

$$tst(\hat{\phi}_i|\hat{\alpha}) = \frac{\hat{\delta}_i - d_{1,i}(\hat{\alpha})}{std(\hat{\phi}_i|\hat{\alpha})}, \tag{2.21}$$

where $std(\hat{\phi}_i|\hat{\alpha})$ denotes the square root of the ith diagonal element of $V_1(\hat{\alpha})$, as defined in equation (2.13). Actually, we intend to systematically adopt this individual coefficients encompassing approach in the remainder of this book.

2.4.4 Nesting and Encompassing

There is occasional ambiguity in the encompassing literature regarding the interaction between nesting and encompassing. On the one hand, Hendry and Richard (1989, 408) assert that "if M_2 is nested within M_1, then M_1 automatically encompasses M_2 at least in the population sense of definition 2 since sampling fluctuations could still occasionally result in M_1 failing to parameterically encompass M_2." On the other hand, Gouriéroux and Monfort (1995, proposition 8, 203 and example 3.1, 204) show that "A model M_2 nesting a model M_1 does not necessarily encompass M_1" (note the index permutation) and provide a linear example subject to inequality constraints. They further clarify that "The previous proposition is surprising because it is counterintuitive and is contrary to what is often said in the literature. Mathematically, a larger model will encompass a smaller one if we can apply a theorem of iterated projections. Therefore, the intuitive implication is valid for Gaussian linear models with linear constraints on the parameters. It is this example that is often presented in the literature." See also Dhaene (1997, proposition 4, 41).

Actually, it appears that much of the confusion originates from a surprising finding that formal generic definitions of nesting are often missing from econometric textbooks and/or presented only through mostly linear examples. The definition that we follow in this book is that offered by Gouriéroux and Monfort (1995, example 2.12, 199), in which $D \subset A$, where D and A represent the respective parameter spaces of $M_2(\delta)$ and $M_1(\alpha)$. It is easy to modify figures 2.1

and 2.2 to accommodate nesting (just enlarge A and shrink D to the point where $D \subset A$, leaving θ outside A). Indeed, under that generic definition, nesting does not imply encompassing.

Hendry and Richard (1989) do not formally define nesting but, from their comments and examples, it would appear that they are implicitly considering cases where there is a function h from A to D such that

$$\hat{\delta} = h(\hat{\alpha}) + \hat{e}, \tag{2.22}$$

where $\text{plim}\,\hat{e} = 0$. It follows that

$$\delta_1(\alpha) \equiv h(\alpha), \text{ and } \hat{\phi} = \hat{\delta} - \delta_1(\hat{\alpha}) = \hat{e}, \tag{2.23}$$

to the effect that M_1 HMR encompasses M_2 (at least asymptotically).

In this book, we present three cases where M_2 is nested within M_1: the linear example 2.9.1, when $M_X Z = 0$; the nonlinear example 2.9.2, and foremost, the timber auction application in chapter 6. It is only in the first case that nesting implies encompassing.

As we discussed in section 2.2.4 in the context of linear dynamic models, parsimonious encompassing, whereby a nested model M_2 encompasses a larger nesting model M_1, is an important component of a model reduction strategy, whereby an initial overparameterized model M_1 is sequentially reduced by the application of parsimonious encompassing F-tests. See Hendry (1995, section 14.6) and Hendry and Doornik (2014). In the context of linear models, where nesting implies encompassing, if M_2 is nested within M_1 and parsimoniously encompasses M_1, then M_1 and M_2 mutually encompass each other.

The concept of parsimonious encompassing has also been formalized by Gouriéroux and Monfort (1995, section 3.1), who define asymptotic parsimonious encompassing as follows: "If M_2 is nested in M_1 and encompasses M_1, M_2 and M_1 are at the same distance of f_{oy} and M_2 is more parsimonious" (f_{oy} denotes the underlying DGP probability density function, and we permuted the subscripts 1 and 2 for compatibility with our notation). Being "at the same distance of f_{oy}" represents the asymptotic definition of mutual encompassing.

2.5 Finite Sample Encompassing

In sections 2.5 and 2.6, we momentarily present our version of encompassing within a likelihood framework to facilitate explicit comparisons with HMR and DGM. Starting with section 2.7 and in the subsequent chapters, we shall move away from this loglikelihood-based presentation of encompassing and adopt instead a far more operational, simulation-based concept of encompassing that relies on MSM estimation (or any alternative operational estimation procedure) and simulated finite sample distributions, in line with our initial objective (as discussed in chapter 1) of providing an operational encompassing procedure that can be applied to complex empirical applications.

Within this momentary loglikelihood framework, there are three basic premises to the following approach that we propose:

1. As discussed in section 2.3, we do not intend to test M_1 against M_2. Instead, we want to find out whether our preferred model M_1 could be improved further to address eventual failures to encompass M_2.
2. Further, as discussed in chapter 1, neither are we interested in testing whether $M_1(\alpha)$ represents the underlying DGP since we know beforehand that it does not do so in any policy relevant empirical applications. Instead, we propose to return to the foundational concept of encompassing, which is that of whether $M_1(\hat{\alpha})$ can account for $\hat{\delta}$.
3. Relatedly, as discussed in chapter 1, our approach relies exclusively on simulated finite sampling distributions derived under $M_1(\hat{\alpha})$, *as estimated*, not an asymptotic extension thereof.
4. Instead of computing an aggregate WET statistic, we propose to compute encompassing *t*-statistics for each individual component of $\hat{\delta}$, as well as for any other M_2 statistic that might be of interest to the owner of M_1. This will enable one to identify eventual specific encompassing failures, thereby providing critical guidance for further improvements of $M_1(\hat{\alpha})$ in the direction of $M_2(\hat{\delta})$.

To meet these objectives, we replace H_0^{HMR} in equation (2.15) by the weaker hypothesis:

$$H_0 : \mathbb{E}(\hat{\phi}|M_1(\hat{\alpha})) = 0, \tag{2.24}$$

which represents our interpretation of $M_1(\hat{\alpha})$ accounts for $\hat{\delta}$. Note a key difference between H_0^{HMR} and H_0, as defined in equations (2.15) and (2.24), respectively. Specifically, H_0^{HMR} relies on asymptotic convergence under $M_1(\alpha)$, not $M_1(\hat{\alpha})$, though obviously, once the asymptotic moments in equations (2.8) and (2.10) obtain, the unknown α will need to be replaced ex-post by $\hat{\alpha}$. In sharp contrast, H_0 represents a finite sample definition conditional on $\hat{\alpha}$, as estimated from the actual sample (which summarizes the available information at the time when policy interpretations and/or recommendations are to be made). This key distinction is discussed further in section 2.6. Verifying whether H_0 obtains requires computing the sampling distribution of $\hat{\delta}$ under $M_1(\hat{\alpha})$ and checking whether each component of $\hat{\delta}$ falls within its $M_1(\hat{\alpha})$ confidence interval. Specifically, let $\hat{\delta}_i$ denote the *i*th individual component of $\hat{\delta}$. Let

$$d_{1,i}(\hat{\alpha}) = \mathbb{E}[\hat{\delta}_i | M_1(\hat{\alpha})] \tag{2.25}$$

$$std(\hat{\delta}_i | \hat{\alpha}) = \text{Std}[\hat{\delta}_i | M_1(\hat{\alpha})]. \tag{2.26}$$

The corresponding t statistic for $\hat{\delta}_i$ is then given by

$$tst(\hat{\delta}_i | \hat{\alpha}) = \frac{\hat{\delta}_i - d_{1,i}(\hat{\alpha})}{std(\hat{\delta}_i | \hat{\alpha})}. \tag{2.27}$$

Comparing $tst(\hat{\delta}_i | \hat{\alpha})$ with $tst(\hat{\phi}_i | \hat{\alpha})$, as defined in equation (2.21), we note that both statistics share the same numerator. Momentarily referring to the DGM asymptotic framework in section 2.4.2, we note that the plim of this common numerator under $M_0(\theta)$ is given by

$$\underset{M_0(\theta)}{\text{plim}}[\hat{\delta}_i - d_{1,i}(\hat{\alpha})] = \delta_{0,i}(\theta) - \delta_{1,i}(\alpha_0(\theta)), \tag{2.28}$$

which, as shown by DGM, will be different from zero if $M_1(\hat{\alpha})$ does not converge to the unknown DGP $M_0(\theta)$. On the other hand, equation (2.9) implies that asymptotically,

$$\text{Var}(\sqrt{N}\hat{\delta}_N | M_1(\alpha)) > \text{Var}(\sqrt{N}\hat{\phi}_N | M_1(\alpha)). \tag{2.29}$$

We expect this inequality to hold in finite samples due to the covariance between $\hat{\delta}$ and $d_1(\hat{\alpha})$, as illustrated in examples 2.9.1 and 2.9.2.

Therefore,

$$|tst(\hat{\phi}_i | \hat{\alpha})| > |tst(\hat{\delta}_i | \hat{\alpha})|, \tag{2.30}$$

which confirms our earlier assertion that H_0 is necessary but not sufficient for H_0^{HMR}. Therefore, it could happen that H_0^{HMR} would be rejected, even though H_0 would not. This is not a problem for serious empirical applications, where H_0 ("account for") is all we need in order to validate policy analyses derived under $M_1(\hat{\alpha})$.

2.6 Summary

The DGM approach is conceptually important since, in particular, it highlights the asymptotic behavior of the encompassing difference in the empirically relevant situation when the unknown DGP $M_0(\theta)$ is not in $\mathcal{M}_1$, as illustrated in figure 2.2. However, it is not operational for serious empirical applications.

In contrast, as we shall see, it is straightforward to implement finite sample versions of both H_0 and H_0^{HMR}, as defined in equations (2.24) and (2.15), respectively. Therefore, in this summary, we compare H_0 and H_0^{HMR}, allowing for any consistent estimation of the modeler's choice. Full MSM-based simulation implementations will be discussed in chapter 5.

- Under both approaches, the encompassing difference is defined as

$$\hat{\phi} = \hat{\delta} - d_1(\hat{\alpha}), \text{ with} \tag{2.31}$$

$$d_1(\hat{\alpha}) = \mathbb{E}(\hat{\delta}|M_1(\alpha))|_{\alpha=\hat{\alpha}}. \tag{2.32}$$

It follows that $\mathbb{E}(\hat{\phi}|M_1(\alpha))|_{\alpha=\hat{\alpha}} = 0$.

- The key difference comes from the respective covariance matrix (or individual standard deviations) used to assess whether $\hat{\phi}$ (or $\hat{\phi}_i$) significantly differs from zero, which obtains as follows:
  1. Conforming to equation (2.24), H_0 relies on the *marginal* distribution of $\hat{\delta}$ given $M_1(\hat{\alpha})$, from which that of $\hat{\phi} = \hat{\delta} - \delta_1(\hat{\alpha})$ obtains.
  2. Conforming to equation (2.15), H_0^{HMR} relies on the *joint* distribution of $(\hat{\alpha}, \hat{\delta})$ given $M_1(\alpha)$, from which that of $\hat{\phi}$ obtains from equation (2.31). In practice, since α is unknown, it will be replaced ex-post by $\hat{\alpha}$.

To highlight further that key difference, we restate it in terms of auxiliary MC simulations. Full details of this process will be provided in chapter 5. Under both H_0 and H_0^{HMR}, we first produce a set of S_2 simulated samples from $M_1(\hat{\alpha})$, such as $\{\tilde{y}_j\}_{j=1}^{S_2}$. We shall subsequently refer to this round of simulation as an "outer loop" to distinguish it from the eventual "inner loop" used for MSM estimation.

1. Under H_0, the simulated samples are used to compute the corresponding set of simulated estimates of δ, such as $\{\tilde{\delta}_j\}_{j=1}^{S_2}$. MC estimates of the conditional mean and covariance matrix of $\hat{\delta}$ obtains as

$$\tilde{d}_1(\hat{\alpha}) = \frac{1}{S_2}\sum_{j=1}^{S_2} \tilde{\delta}_j, \tag{2.33}$$

$$\tilde{V}(\hat{\delta}|M_1(\hat{\alpha})) = \frac{1}{S_2}\sum_{j=1}^{S_2} [\tilde{\delta}_j - \tilde{d}_1(\hat{\alpha})][\tilde{\delta}_j - \tilde{d}_1(\hat{\alpha})]', \tag{2.34}$$

from which one computes a global χ^2 statistic or individual t-statistics as in equation (2.27).

2. Under H_0^{HMR}, the simulated samples are used to compute the corresponding set of simulated estimates of *both* α and δ, such as $\{\tilde{\alpha}_j, \tilde{\delta}_j\}_{j=1}^{S_2}$. The corresponding MC draws of $\hat{\phi}$ are then given by

$$\tilde{\phi}_j = \tilde{\delta}_j - d_1(\tilde{\alpha}_j), \quad j : 1 \to S_2. \tag{2.35}$$

A major complication arises from the fact that we typically will not have an analytical expression for $d_1(\tilde{\alpha}_j)$. In such a case, for *each* $\tilde{\alpha}_j$, we need an auxiliary set of MC simulations to estimate $d_1(\tilde{\alpha}_j)$. Specifically, for each $\tilde{\alpha}_j$, we draw S_3 auxiliary samples $\{\tilde{y}_{j,k}\}_{k=1}^{S_3}$ from $M_1(\tilde{\alpha}_j)$, from which we compute the corresponding sequence of $\hat{\delta}$ estimates, such as $\{\tilde{\delta}_{j,k}\}_{k=1}^{S_3}$. The corresponding MC estimate of $d_1(\tilde{\alpha}_j)$ obtains as

$$\tilde{d}_1(\tilde{\alpha}_j) = \frac{1}{S_3}\sum_{k=1}^{S_3}\tilde{\delta}_{j,k}, \quad j: 1 \to S_2, \tag{2.36}$$

which is then substituted for $d_1(\tilde{\alpha}_j)$ in equation (2.35). MC estimates of the conditional mean and covariance matrix of $\hat{\phi}$ obtain as

$$\tilde{\phi}_1(\hat{\alpha}) = \frac{1}{S_2}\sum_{j=1}^{S_2}\tilde{\phi}_j \tag{2.37}$$

$$\tilde{V}_1(\hat{\phi}|M_1(\hat{\alpha})) = \frac{1}{S_2}\sum_{j=1}^{S_2}[\tilde{\phi}_j - \tilde{\phi}_1(\hat{\alpha})][\tilde{\phi}_j - \tilde{\phi}_1(\hat{\alpha})]'. \tag{2.38}$$

We have seen in equation (2.29) that

$$\tilde{V}_1(\hat{\phi}|M_1(\hat{\alpha})) < \tilde{V}_1(\hat{\delta}|M_1(\hat{\alpha})), \tag{2.39}$$

at least asymptotically. As highlighted in examples 2.9.1 and 2.9.2, it is generally expected to hold under finite samples due to the covariance between $\hat{\alpha}$ and $\hat{\delta}$. It follows that H_0^{HMR} is sufficient but not necessary for H_0 encompassing. Therefore, a finding that H_0^{HMR} is rejected does not imply that M_1 cannot be used for policy analysis (which only requires H_0).

3. As discussed in section 2.3, M_2 would generally not be considered as a potential alternative for M_1. Instead, it is meant to be used for either validation of M_1 or, in case of a failure to encompass, to suggest eventual further improvement of M_1 in the direction of M_2. Obviously, in view of the typically large sunk costs in the estimation of M_1, its owner would want to avoid additional extensive computations associated with M_2. This would be the case if M_2 happened to represent a counterfactual nested version of M_1. This is the case for the timber auction application presented in chapter 6, where M_2 represents a non collusive version of M_1. In such cases, estimation of M_2 obtains directly from constrained estimation of M_1.

   When M_2 represents a model produced by other researchers, the best case scenario would be that when the owner of M_1 has access to the estimation program–and eventual additional data–used by the owner of M_2 (a necessary condition for replicability, but unfortunately one that is not universal in economics). This is why, while we advocate the use of MSM for estimation, our presentation of simulation encompassing in chapter 5 allows alternative estimation methods for the models under consideration.

2.7 Feasibility

Both DGM and HMR encompassing are based upon a ML framework, which could also, conceptually at least, apply to the finite sample concept of encompassing introduced in section 2.5. Three points are noteworthy in this regard:

1. The theoretical advantage offered by that approach under DGM and HMR is that one can rely upon powerful asymptotic, loglikelihood-based tools to derive the relevant limiting distributions. However, it turns out to be a major numerical as well as conceptual obstacle to loglikelihood-based implementations of encompassing in most nonlinear applications. Specifically, major empirical applications such as the timber auction application in chapter 6 are far too complex to allow the specification of an operational loglikelihood function and for the subsequent computation of ML estimators.

   This is why, in chapter 5, we shall implement MSM-based versions of encompassing that require only that the models under consideration be amenable to MC simulations (actually, the approach that we shall present is applicable to any consistent estimation technique under the same minimal condition).
2. Relatedly, the loglikelihood-based concepts required for DGM and HMR encompassing (KLIC, pseudo-true values, and binding functions) will all be replaced by MSM-based finite versions thereof, here again, applicable to any consistent estimation technique.
3. A loglikelihood approach implicitly relies on the infinite sequence of moments associated with the assumed distribution. It is maximally efficient under an axiom of "correct specification," but it lacks robustness against empirically unavoidable specification errors. It makes it very difficult to differentiate among the empirically most critical assumptions and all the additional auxiliary assumptions (e.g., normality) required for a full loglikelihood specification. It also makes it difficult to distinguish between important and accessory potential encompassing failures.

Perhaps the most critical advantage of the MSM approach that we propose here is that, beyond its broad numerical feasibility, it allows the modeler to specifically select the essential moments that need to be encompassed to validate policy conclusions derived from the estimated model. This critial issue is discussed further in section 4.3.1.

2.8 Exogeneity

Most empirical applications include exogenous variables. The relevant concept is that of "weak exogeneity," as defined in Engle, Hendry and Richard (1983). It essentially assumes the absence of restrictions between the parameters of the conditional model of interest and those of the unspecified marginal process for the conditioning exogenous variables. That assumption allows for efficient estimation of the conditional model without having to specify the marginal exogenous process.

As emphasized by Gouriéroux and Monfort (1995, section 4.5), the presence of exogenous variables raises an immediate problem for the derivation of the asymptotic concepts of KLIC distances, pseudo-true values, and binding functions since they obviously depend on the unspecified exogenous process.

Therefore, in the remainder of this book, starting with the examples in section 2.9, we shall only consider finite sample versions of the concepts of pseudo-true values and binding functions, all of which will be estimated by MC simulations conditional upon the observed exogenous variables.

2.9 Examples

2.9.1 Linear Example

Let all three models be linear regressions:

$$M_0(\theta): y = W\theta + u_0, \qquad \theta \in R^p \tag{2.40}$$

$$M_1(\alpha): y = X\alpha + u_1, \qquad \alpha \in R^k \tag{2.41}$$

$$M_2(\delta): y = Z\delta + u_2, \qquad \delta \in R^l, \tag{2.42}$$

where $u_i \sim N(0, \sigma_i^2 I)$. For the ease of exposition, we assume that the σ_i^2 values are known (under ordinary least squares (OLS) estimation $\text{plim}(\hat{\sigma}_i^2/\sigma_i^2) = 1$). For meaningful comparisons, we need a common probability space. Therefore, all three models are interpreted as being conditional on the column space of (W, X, Z) and correspond to different conditional independence assumptions.

Eventual linear relationships between the columns of (W, X, Z) are handled through the use of generalized inverse and degrees of freedom corrections as needed.

Estimation is by OLS and, as explained in section 2.4.3, asymptotic pseudo-true values and binding functions are replaced by the corresponding finite sample expected values, conditional on $(X\ W\ Z)$. Therefore:

$$\hat{\alpha} = (X'X)^{-1}X'Y, \qquad \alpha_0(\theta) = (X'X)^{-1}X'W\theta \tag{2.43}$$

$$\hat{\delta} = (Z'Z)^{-1}Z'\,Y, \qquad \delta_0(\theta) = (Z'Z)^{-1}Z'W\theta \tag{2.44}$$

$$\delta_1(\alpha) = (Z'Z)^{-1}Z'X\alpha. \tag{2.45}$$

Equations (2.43) to (2.45) enable us to compare the three versions of encompassing introduced in sections 2.4 and 2.5 as follows:

1. **DGM encompassing**: the finite sample version of the DGM condition in equation (2.4) is given by

$$\delta_0(\theta) - \delta_1(\alpha_0(\theta)) = (Z'Z)^{-1}Z'M_X W\theta = 0. \tag{2.46}$$

It follows that there are two scenarios for $M_1(\alpha)$ to DGM-encompass $M_2(\delta)$.

- **Scenario 1**: $M_X W$=0, (2.47)

which implies the (rather unusual) condition that $M_0(\theta)$ is nested within $M_1(\alpha)$; that is, that $M_1(\alpha)$ is overparameterized. Actually, in view of our generic definition of nesting in equation (2.22), we only need equation (2.47) to hold in expectation. Thus, equation (2.47) can be replaced by the more general condition that there is a $k \times p$ matrix B with $p \leq k$ such that

$$W = XB + V_0, \tag{2.48}$$

with V_0 denoting a matrix of regression residuals. It follows that the DGP $M_0(\theta)$ in equation (2.40) can be rewritten as

$$y = XB\theta + (u_0 + V_0\theta) = XB\theta + v_0. \tag{2.49}$$

It then follows that

$$\alpha_0(\theta) = B\theta, \qquad \delta_0(\theta) = (Z'Z)^{-1}Z'XB\theta, \tag{2.50}$$

which, together with equation (2.45), implies that DGM condition (2.46) is satisfied. Note that since y is actually generated by $M_0(\theta)$, the OLS estimate of α would satisfy in expectation the restriction built into $M_0(\theta)$. But again, this appears to be a rather unusual scenario.

- **Scenario 2**: $M_X Z{=}0,$ (2.51)

which implies that $M_2(\delta)$ is nested within $M_1(\alpha)$. Here again, a more general version of condition (2.51) is that there is a $k \times l$ matrix A with $l \leq k$ such that

$$Z = XA + V_2, \tag{2.52}$$

in which case $M_2(\delta)$ can be rewritten as

$$y = XA\delta + (u_2 + V_2\delta). \tag{2.53}$$

It follows that

$$\delta_0(\theta) = (A'X'XA)^{-1}A'X'W\theta, \qquad \delta_1(\alpha) = (A'X'XA)^{-1}A'X'X\alpha, \tag{2.54}$$

which, together with equation (2.43), implies that the DGM condition (2.46) is satisfied. However, note that, as discussed in section 2.4.4, this linear example represents a situation where nesting does imply encompassing, regardless of whether $M_1(\alpha)$ is the DGP.

2. **HMR encompassing**: HMR relies on the encompassing difference:

$$\hat{\phi} = \hat{\delta} - \delta_1(\hat{\alpha}) = (Z'Z)^{-1}Z'M_X y. \tag{2.55}$$

As explained in section 2.6, the distribution of $\hat{\phi}$ is derived under $M_1(\alpha)$, so $M_0(\theta)$ is actually not in play. The finite sample mean vector and covariance matrix of $\hat{\phi}$ under $M_1(\alpha)$ are given by

$$\mathbb{E}(\hat{\phi}|M_1(\alpha)) = (Z'Z)^{-1}Z'M_X X\alpha = 0, \tag{2.56}$$

$$V_1(\hat{\phi}|M_1(\alpha)) = \sigma_1^2 (Z'Z)^{-1}Z'M_X Z(Z'Z)^{-1}. \tag{2.57}$$

The corresponding HMR WET statistic is given by

$$\eta_W^{HMR} = \frac{1}{\sigma_1^2} y'M_X Z(Z'M_X Z)^{+} Z'M_X y \sim \chi^2(d), \tag{2.58}$$

where d denotes the rank of $Z'M_X Z$, and $(Z'M_X Z)^{+}$ its generalized inverse. Obviously, if $M_X Z = 0$, it follows that $\hat{\phi}$ is identically zero conditional on $M_1(\alpha)$.

As discussed in HMR, the test statistic in equation (2.58) is also that which obtains for the "choice of regressors" problem under the maintained hypothesis $\{M_1, M_2\}$.

3. **Encompassing**: As explained in sections 2.5 and 2.6, the relevant distribution is that of $\hat{\delta}$ conditionally on $M_1(\hat{\alpha})$, with

$$d_1(\hat{\alpha}) = \mathbb{E}[\hat{\delta}|M_1(\hat{\alpha})] = (Z'Z)^{-1}Z'X\hat{\alpha}. \tag{2.59}$$

Since

$$\hat{\delta} - d_1(\hat{\alpha}) = (Z'Z)^{-1}Z'(y - X\hat{\alpha}), \tag{2.60}$$

it follows that

$$V_1[\hat{\delta}|M_1(\hat{\alpha})] = \sigma_1^2(Z'Z)^{-1}. \tag{2.61}$$

It follows from equations (2.55) and (2.61) that the WET encompassing test statistic is given by

$$\begin{aligned} \eta_W &= \frac{1}{\sigma_1^2}(y - X\hat{\alpha})'Z(Z'Z)^{-1}Z'(y - X\hat{\alpha}) \\ &= \frac{1}{\sigma_1^2}y'M_X Z(Z'Z)^{-1}Z'M_X y \sim \chi^2(l). \end{aligned} \tag{2.62}$$

Note that

$$Z'Z > Z'M_X Z \tag{2.63}$$

conforming with the more general inequality in equation (2.29). It follows that $\eta_W^{HMR} > \eta_W$, with the respective degrees of freedom l and $d \leq l$.

2.9.2 Nonlinear Example

The following one-parameter mixture example serves two main objectives:

1. To illustrate how encompassing can be applied with consistent moment estimators being used in place of analytically intractable ML estimators
2. To highlight further the fundamental difference between H_0 and H_0^{HMR}

In this section, we first derive analytical results and then provide a nested, numerical illustration. The simulated version of this example will be presented in section 4.5, after we introduce simulation encompassing.

Let the unknown DGP be the mixture model:

$$M_0(\theta): y = \begin{cases} u_i^0 & \text{proba } 1 - p_i \\ \theta x_i + u_i^0 & \text{proba } p_i, \end{cases} \tag{2.64}$$

where $\{x_i\}_{i=1}^N$ denotes a vector of observed exogenous variables, $\{p_i\}_{i=1}^N$ denotes a vector of unobserved non-stochastic probabilities, and the u_i^0 values are independent and identically distributed (i.i.d.) $N(0, \sigma^2)$.

Let's assume that we construct a vector $\{q_i\}_{i=1}^N$ of observable non-stochastic proxies for the unknown p_i. The model of interest M_1 is defined as

$$M_1(\alpha): y_i = \begin{cases} u_i^1 & \text{proba } 1 - q_i \\ \alpha x_i + u_i^1 & \text{proba } q_i. \end{cases} \tag{2.65}$$

The counterfactual model M_2 to be encompassed is defined as

$$M_2(\delta): y_i = \delta x_i + u_i^2. \tag{2.66}$$

For simplicity, we assume that the values of u_i^1 and u_i^2 are also i.i.d. $N(0, \sigma^2)$, with σ^2 known.[1] We note that both $M_0(\theta)$ and $M_1(\alpha)$ represent non-stochastic mixtures of Normal distributions. It follows that a loglikelihood-based derivation of pseudo-true values, binding functions, and encompassing statistics would be complicated, whether analytically or numerically (and even more so for the timber auction application presented in chapter 6, which involves stochastic mixtures).

An operational alternative to ML consists of using a consistent moment estimator (actually OLS) for $\mathbb{E}(y_i|x_i)$. The corresponding least squares estimators of α and δ are given by

$$\widehat{\alpha} = \frac{\sum q_i x_i y_i}{\sum q_i^2 x_i^2}, \quad \widehat{\delta} = \frac{\sum x_i y_i}{\sum x_i^2}. \tag{2.67}$$

Note that at this expository stage, p_i and q_i are not parameterized. In the numerical illustration given next, we shall introduce an auxiliary parameterization for p_i and q_i as functions of the x_i. It will imply that M_2 is nested within M_1. However, since M_0 and M_1 will be nonlinear under this augmented parameterization, nesting no longer implies encompassing, as discussed in section 2.4.4. The same will be true for the timber auction application in chapter 6.

In the absence of loglikelihood functions and of assumptions on the exogenous $\{x_i\}$ process, we replace the loglikelihood-based definitions of pseudo-true values and binding functions in equations (2.2) and (2.3) by their finite sample counterparts:

$$\alpha_0(\theta) = \mathbb{E}[\hat{\alpha}|M_0(\theta)] = \theta \frac{\sum p_i q_i x_i^2}{\sum q_i^2 x_i^2} \tag{2.68}$$

$$\delta_0(\theta) = \mathbb{E}[\hat{\delta}|M_0(\theta)] = \theta \frac{\sum p_i x_i^2}{\sum x_i^2}. \tag{2.69}$$

$$\delta_1(\alpha) = \mathbb{E}[\hat{\delta}|M_1(\alpha)] = \alpha \frac{\sum q_i x_i^2}{\sum x_i^2}. \tag{2.70}$$

The encompassing difference is given by

$$\hat{\phi} = \hat{\delta} - \delta_1(\hat{\alpha}) = \hat{\delta} - \hat{\alpha} \frac{\sum q_i x_i^2}{\sum x_i^2}. \tag{2.71}$$

The finite sample counterpart of the DGM asymptotic condition in equation (2.4) is given by

$$\phi_0(\theta) = \delta_0(\theta) - \delta_1(\alpha_0(\theta)) = \theta\Big[\frac{\sum p_i x_i^2}{\sum x_i^2} - \frac{\sum p_i q_i x_i^2}{\sum q_i^2 x_i^2} \cdot \frac{\sum q_i x_i^2}{\sum x_i^2}\Big]. \quad (2.72)$$

It immediately follows that $\phi_0(\theta) \neq 0$ unless $p_i \equiv q_i, i : 1 \to N$. The expectation of $\hat{\phi}$ given $M_1(\alpha)$ is expressed by

$$\mathbb{E}[\hat{\phi}|M_1(\alpha)] = \delta_1(\alpha) - \delta_1(\alpha) = 0, \quad (2.73)$$

regardless of whether or not $q_i = p_i, i : 1 \to N$. Obviously, if the q_i were different from the p_i, then $\hat{\phi}$ would not converge to zero; since the data is generated by $M_0(\theta)$, not by $M_1(\alpha)$, and H_0^{HMR}, would then be asymptotically rejected.

In this simple example, we can derive analytical expectations for relevant t-statistics (see appendix 2B).

- The HMR encompassing t-statistic is given by

$$tst(\hat{\phi}|\hat{\alpha}) = \frac{\hat{\delta} - \delta_1(\hat{\alpha})}{std(\hat{\phi}|\hat{\alpha})}, \text{ where} \quad (2.74)$$

$$std(\hat{\phi}|\hat{\alpha}) = \Big[\sum_i (\phi_i - \gamma\psi_i)^2 v_i^2\Big]^{1/2}, \text{ with} \quad (2.75)$$

$$\phi_i = \frac{x_i}{\sum x_i^2}, \qquad \psi_i = \frac{q_i x_i}{\sum q_i^2 x_i^2}, \qquad \gamma = \frac{\sum q_i x_i}{\sum x_i^2}, \text{ and} \quad (2.76)$$

$$v_i^2 = \sigma^2 + q_i(1 - q_i)\hat{\alpha}^2 x_i^2. \quad (2.77)$$

- The encompassing t-statistic in equation (2.27) is given by

$$tst(\hat{\delta}|\hat{\alpha}) = \frac{\hat{\delta} - \delta_1(\hat{\alpha})}{std(\hat{\delta}|\hat{\alpha})}, \text{ where} \quad (2.78)$$

$$std(\hat{\delta}|\hat{\alpha}) = (\sum_i \phi_i^2 v_i^2)^{1/2}. \quad (2.79)$$

As expected, $std(\hat{\delta}|\hat{\alpha}) > std(\hat{\phi}|\hat{\alpha})$ is the result of a positive covariance between $\hat{\alpha}$ and $\hat{\alpha}$ under $M_1(\alpha)$ (see appendix 2B).

Numerical Illustration

For illustration, we consider the following setup:

- The x_i are i.i.d. draws from a lognormal (μ, ω^2), whose mean and standard deviation are given by

$$m = \mathbb{E}(X) = e^{\mu + \frac{1}{2}\omega^2}, \qquad s = m(e^{\omega^2} - 1)^{1/2}. \quad (2.80)$$

- The values of p_i and q_i are one-parameter, monotone-decreasing functions of x, defined as

$$p(x) = \frac{p_0(e^m - 1)}{p_0(e^m - 1) + e^x(1 - p_0)}, \quad p_0 \in (0, 1) \tag{2.81}$$

$$q(x) = \frac{q_0(e^m - 1)}{q_0(e^m - 1) + e^x(1 - q_0)}, \quad q_0 \in (0, 1). \tag{2.82}$$

While this parameterization looks complicated, it is actually easy to interpret:

$$\begin{aligned} &\text{if } x = 0, \text{ then } p(x) = q(x) = 1 \\ &\text{if } x = m, \text{ then } p(x) = p_0 \text{ and } q(x) = q_0 \\ &\text{if } x \to \infty, \text{ then } p(x) \text{ and } q(x) \to 0. \end{aligned} \tag{2.83}$$

It also offers the advantage that $M_2(\delta)$ is now nested within $M_1(\alpha)$ since it is obtained by setting $q_0 = 1$, in which case all $q_i = 1$.

For illustration, we set (θ, σ, m, s) to be equal to $(0.3, 0.1, 5, 3)$. The sample size is set at 1,000. The x sample is drawn from the log-normal distribution with parameters $\mu = 1.456$ and $\omega = 0.555$ obtained from (m, s) using equation (2.80). Around 91.6 percent of the x draws lie in the interval [0, 9]. As for p_0, we considered two scenarios: one with $p_0 = 0.75$ (with $p(7) = 0.288$) and the other with $p_0 = 0.95$ (with $p(7) = 0.719$).

Conditionally on the x and p_0, the y is then drawn from $M_0(\theta)$. For each of the two p_0 scenarios, we select five values of q_0 differing from p_0 by 0.0, 0.05, 0.10, 0.15, and 0.20, respectively.

The results are reported in columns 3 to 9 of table 2.1. They were produced analytically using equation (2.67) for $(\hat{\alpha}, \hat{\delta})$ and equations (2.79), (2.78), (2.75), and (2.74) for the H_0 and H_0^{HMR} results.

Note that so long as p_0 is kept fixed, and since we rely on a common seed for the random draws of x and y under $M_0(\theta)$, the sample (x, y) remains the same across the first five and last five rows of table 2.1, and so does $\hat{\delta}$, the OLS estimator of y on x.

In accordance with equations (2.39), (2.75), and (2.79), we find that $std(\hat{\phi}|\hat{\alpha}) < std(\hat{\delta}|\hat{\alpha})$, and therefore, $|tst(\hat{\phi}|\hat{\alpha})| > |tst(\hat{\delta}|\hat{\alpha})|$, with the difference between the two being an increasing function of the distance between q_0 and p_0. It also follows that, as discussed in section 2.6, there are q_0 intervals for which H_0 remains accepted, while H_0^{HMR} is rejected.

An interesting result from table 2.1 is that it appears to be easier to detect M_1 misspecification when q_0 underestimates the actual p_0 (last five rows) than in the opposite case (top five rows).

Table 2.1
Encompassing results (example)

					H_0		H_0^{HMR}	
p_0	q_0	$\hat{\alpha}$	$\hat{\delta}$	$\delta_1(\hat{\alpha})$	$std(\hat{\delta}\|\hat{\alpha})$	$tst(\hat{\delta}\|\hat{\alpha})$	$std(\hat{\phi}\|\hat{\alpha})$	$tst(\hat{\phi}\|\hat{\alpha})$
0.75	0.75	0.305	0.102	0.101	0.0034	0.247	0.0020	0.414
0.75	0.80	0.288	0.102	0.104	0.0033	−0.539	0.0020	−0.911
0.75	0.85	0.270	0.102	0.107	0.0032	−1.363	0.0019	−2.327
0.75	0.90	0.249	0.102	0.109	0.0031	−2.240	0.0018	−3.883
0.75	0.95	0.219	0.102	0.111	0.0029	−3.163	0.0016	−5.663
0.95	0.95	0.302	0.154	0.153	0.0040	0.282	0.0022	0.505
0.95	0.90	0.330	0.154	0.145	0.0041	2.293	0.0024	3.983
0.95	0.85	0.350	0.154	0.138	0.0042	3.896	0.0024	6.598
0.95	0.80	0.367	0.154	0.133	0.0042	5.188	0.0025	8.786
0.95	0.75	0.382	0.154	0.127	0.0042	6.386	0.0025	10.71

2.10 Generalizations

As pointed out by Mizon and Richard (1986, equation (2.12)), one might wish to test for encompassing M_2-statistics that are not functions of $\hat{\delta}$ only. An example is provided in chapter 6, where we also test whether $M_1(\hat{\alpha})$ can encompass the MSM fit of $M_2(\hat{\delta})$. Another important example is that of "forecast encompassing," which will be discussed in chapter 3. Under a finite sample, let

$$\hat{b} = b(Y;\hat{\delta}) \tag{2.84}$$

denote an M_2-statistic that depends not only on $\hat{\delta}$ but also on a subset of the actual data Y. Here again, it is important to distinguish between H_0^{HMR} and H_0, as discussed in sections 2.4 and 2.5, respectively. Both approaches rely upon the generalized encompassing difference:

$$\hat{\phi} = b(Y;\hat{\delta}) - d_1(\hat{\alpha}), \text{ where} \tag{2.85}$$

$$d_1(\hat{\alpha}) = \mathbb{E}[b(Y;\hat{\delta})|M_1(\hat{\alpha})]. \tag{2.86}$$

As discussed in section 2.6, the critical difference lies in the computation of the covariance matrix to be used to construct individual encompassing t-statistics or overall χ^2-statistics.

1. Under H_0^{HMR}, one relies on finite sample approximations of the asymptotic covariance matrix of $\hat{\phi}$ given $M_1(\alpha)$.
2. Under H_0, one relies instead on the conditional covariance matrix of $b(Y;\hat{\delta})$ given $M_1(\hat{\alpha})$.

Notes:

1. Under HMR, Mizon and Richard (1986) show that through the choice of the statistic $b(Y;\hat{\delta})$, it is possible to generate a wide range of commonly used test statistics and thereby gain further insight into the relationship between Cox, Wald, likelihood ratio, and Lagrange multiplier test statistics. This is representative of the DGM and HMR reliance on encompassing to provide a unified framework for interpreting these various testing approaches. While theoretically important, such a discussion is not a concern of ours in this book, because it focuses on substantive empirical applications.
2. This generalized approach has also been used by Spanos, Hendry and Reade (2008) in the form of a mis-specification encompassing analysis of the linear (M_2) versus nonlinear (M_1) unit root models. Specifically, the authors focus their attention on the implications of M_1 for various probabilistic assumptions associated with M_2. See also Ermini and Hendry (2008).

Except for simple models such as examples 2.9.1 and 2.9.2, it will generally be impossible to evaluate analytically, or even numerically, the binding function $d_1(\hat{\alpha})$, as defined in equation (2.86), and/or the relevant covariance matrices. However, it requires only minor adjustments of the simulation algorithm presented in chapter 5 to compute simulated (finite sample) approximations.

As mentioned previously, "forecast encompassing," to be discussed in chapter 3, is obtained by direct application of equations (2.85) and (2.86) to a subset of M_2-forecast errors. This point will be illustrated with applications to examples 2.9.1 and 2.9.2.

Appendix 2A: Iterated Projections

Let $M_1(\alpha)$ and $M_2(\delta)$ be the two linear models introduced in section 2.9.1, with $X=(Z\ X_2)$ and $\alpha'=(\alpha_1'\ \alpha_2')$ so $M_2\subseteq M_1$. The OLS projection of X_2 on Z is given by

$$X_2=Z\hat{\Pi}+\hat{\epsilon},\ \text{with} \tag{2.A.1}$$

$$\hat{\Pi}=(Z'Z)^{-1}Z'X_2, \qquad \hat{\epsilon}=v_2+Z(\Pi-\hat{\Pi}). \tag{2.A.2}$$

It follows that $M_2(\delta)$ can be rewritten as

$$y=Z(\alpha_1+\hat{\Pi}\alpha_2)+(u_1+X_2\hat{\epsilon}), \tag{2.A.3}$$

whence

$$\delta_1(\alpha)=\begin{pmatrix} I_l & \hat{\Pi}\end{pmatrix}\alpha \tag{2.A.4}$$

$$\delta_1(\hat{\alpha})=\begin{pmatrix} I_l & \hat{\Pi}\end{pmatrix}\hat{\alpha}\equiv\hat{\delta}. \tag{2.A.5}$$

Appendix 2B (Example 2.9.2): Encompassing Standard Deviations

Let $M_1 \equiv M_1(\alpha)$ and $\hat{M}_1 = M_1(\hat{\alpha})$. It follows from equations (2.67) and (2.70) that

$$\hat{\alpha} = \sum_i \psi_i y_i, \qquad \hat{\delta} = \sum_i \phi_i y_i, \qquad \text{and } \delta_1(\alpha) = \gamma\alpha, \tag{2.B.1}$$

with

$$\psi_i = \frac{q_i x_i}{\sum q_i^2 x_i^2}, \qquad \phi_i = \frac{x_i}{\sum x_i^2}, \qquad \text{and } \gamma = \frac{\sum q_i x_i}{\sum x_i^2}. \tag{2.B.2}$$

It follows that

$$\mathbb{E}_{M_1}\begin{pmatrix}\hat{\delta}\\ \delta_1(\hat{\alpha})\end{pmatrix} = \alpha\begin{pmatrix}\sum \phi_i q_i x_i\\ \gamma\sum \psi_i q_i x_i\end{pmatrix} = \alpha\begin{pmatrix}\gamma\\ \gamma\end{pmatrix}, \tag{2.B.3}$$

$$\mathbb{E}_{M_1}(\hat{\phi}) = \mathbb{E}_{M_1}(\hat{\delta} - \delta_1(\hat{\alpha})) = 0. \tag{2.B.4}$$

Moreover,

$$\mathbb{E}_{M_1}(y_i) = \alpha q_i x_i$$

$$\mathbb{E}_{M_1}(y_i^2) = (1-q_i)\sigma^2 + q_i(\sigma^2 + \alpha^2 x_i^2) = \sigma^2 + q_i\alpha^2 x_i^2 \tag{2.B.5}$$

$$V_{M_1}(y_i) = \sigma^2 + q_i\alpha^2 x_i^2 - \alpha^2 q_i^2 x_i^2 = \sigma^2 + q_i(1-q_i)\alpha^2 x_i^2 = v_i^2 \tag{2.B.6}$$

$$V_{M_1}(\hat{\delta}) = \sum \phi_i^2 v_i^2. \tag{2.B.7}$$

In equation (2.79), $std(\hat{\delta}|\hat{\alpha})$ is obtained by setting $\alpha = \hat{\alpha}$.

As for HMR, we have the following additional formulas:

$$\mathrm{Cov}_{M_1}(\hat{\delta}, \delta_1(\hat{\alpha})) = Cov_{M_1}(\sum \phi_i y_i, \alpha \sum \psi_i y_i) = \gamma \sum \phi_i \psi_i v_i^2 \tag{2.B.8}$$

$$\mathrm{Var}_{M_1}(\delta_1(\hat{\alpha})) = \gamma^2 \sum \psi_i^2 v_i^2. \tag{2.B.9}$$

In equation (2.75),

$$\mathrm{Var}_{M_1}(\hat{\delta} - \delta_1(\hat{\alpha})) = \sum(\phi_i^2 - 2\gamma\phi_i\psi_i + \gamma^2\psi_i^2)v_i^2 = \sum_i(\phi_i - \gamma\psi_i)^2 v_i^2 \tag{2.B.10}$$

$std(\hat{\phi}|\hat{\alpha})$ in equation (2.75) obtains by setting $\alpha = \hat{\alpha}$.

3

Forecast Encompassing

A common situation, especially in dynamic macromodeling, is one where different researchers or organizations produce alternative forecasts whose respective performances need to be assessed. Note immediately that forecast assessments can be done only "in sample" since it requires comparing actual observations to forecasts thereof. As reviewed in this chapter, a common practice under such circumstances consists of optimally pooling forecasts. Actually, following the pioneering contribution of Chong and Hendry (1986; hereafter CH), the prevalent interpretation of forecast encompassing is closely related to that of pooling forecasts. While it is not per se a direct application of the concept of encompassing analyzed in chapter 2, it nevertheless serves the very same objective, as we shall discuss here.

The chapter is organized as follows: In section 3.1, we review the related literature. CH forecast encompassing is presented in section 3.2, with application to the linear example 2.9.1. in section 3.3, we present our version of forecast encompassing, revisiting examples 2.9.1 and 2.9.2. Section 3.4 concludes the chapter.

3.1 Literature Review

In a pioneering contribution, (Bates and Granger, 1969, pages 451 and 461), reconsider a common practice at the time that consisted of attempting to discover which is the better forecast, accepting it, and discarding the others. The authors (page 451) argue that "this is not a wise procedure if the objective is to make as good a forecast as possible, since the discarded forecast nearly always contains some useful independent information." Actually, this represents the essence of the concept of forecast encompassing, to be discussed next.

The authors construct weighted combinations of a set of available forecasts and provide several criteria to construct good combinations thereof. An application to monthly forecasts of passenger miles flown one period ahead is used to compare alternative weight combinations. The authors' conclusion (page 461) provides a useful introduction to subsequent concepts of forecast encompassing: "If a model of a time series can be accurately specified then it is possible to derive individual forecasts which could not be bettered."

To the best of our knowledge, CH were the first to introduce a formal concept of forecast encompassing that is closely related to the earlier concepts of pooling forecasts constructed from a "composite artificial model." The link to parametric encompassing is justified, according to CH (page 677) as follows: "Note that the *need* to pool forecasts is *prima facie* evidence of a failure to encompass, and if H_1 is an econometric model and H_2 a univariate time-series model (say) then if H_1 does not encompass H_2 it seems highly suggestive of the possibility that H_1 is dynamically misspecified (that being the only information available to H_2)."

The authors derive the asymptotic distributions of two versions of a forecast encompassing test statistic when the baseline model is a first-order, stationary closed system in companion form. Both statistics are asymptotically distributed as noncentral chi-squared (or central under the null). The authors also ran an extensive MC simulation on a 64×64 distributed array processor to construct finite sample "response surfaces," based on Mizon and Hendry (1980). They conclude page (687): "Tests for forecast encompassing and for the existence of long-run relationships, the calculation of forecast confidence intervals and tests based thereon presently seem both feasible and more promising than conventionally used tools."

See also Ericsson (1992, 1993) for further discussion of CH forecast encompassing and its advantages relative to conventional mean square forecast errors (MSFE) comparisons.

Fair and Shiller (1989) compare the informational content of different ex-ante forecasts by regressing the actual change in a variable on ex-ante forecasts of the change. They argue that (page 326): "Testing procedure is similar to the C-test of Davidson and MacKinnon (1981)—which is a special case of the Wald encompassing test of Mizon and Richard (1986)," though with a number of differences (essentially deleting restrictions on the parameters of the auxiliary regressions and requiring that forecasts beginning in period t contains only information through period t-1). Neither is it required that the error terms be identically distributed.

The authors apply their procedure to comparisons of several forecasts of the log real U.S. gross national product, taken four quarters ahead, from 1977–3 to 1986–2. They find (page 331) that their procedure "appears to be a useful alternative to the standard procedure of comparing forecasts by the size of their Root Mean Squared Errors. In many cases our procedure may be able to discriminate better." They also suggest that combining forecasts may be useful, although forecasts inherently have stochastic properties that might change over time.

Clements and Hendry (1993) discuss the inherent limitations of comparing mean square forecast errors (MSFE) which are not invariant under nonsingular scale preserving linear transformations. In contrast, they demonstrate that the forecast encompassing test proposed by CH, as discussed previously, is invariant to such transformations. The authors also demonstrate that forecast encompassing "enables minimum MSFE, whereas MSFE dominance is only necessary for forecast encompassing."

Diebold (1989, page 590) provides an insightful discussion of the relation between forecast combination and forecast encompassing. His view is best summarized by the following two quotes:

> "Again, however, there would appear to be little room for forecast combination within the encompassing paradigm. If a particular model appears misspecified, it is modified until an acceptable specification has been found, from which optimal forecasts follow directly. Forecast combination is readily dismissed; mechanical combination of manifestly incorrect models will never lead us to the truth" . . .
>
> "However, while pooling of forecasts is suboptimal relative to pooling of information sets, it is clear that in many forecasting situations, particularly when deadlines must be met and timely forecasts produced, pooling of information sets is either impossible or prohibitively costly. This pragmatic observation is, entirely, the raison d'être of the forecast combination literature, in which forecasts rather than models are the basic object of analysis, reflecting an assumed inability to combine information sets."

Diebold also emphasizes a critical need to explore further the efficacity of forecast combination.

Ericsson and Marquez (1993) generalize "Chong and Hendry's statistic to include *sets* of *dynamic nonlinear* models with *uncertain* estimated coefficients generating *multistep* forecasts with possibly *systematic* biases." Using MC simulations, the authors apply their generalized statistics to forecasts for 1985–1 to 1987–4 from six models of the U.S. merchandise trade balance.

Perhaps unsurprisingly, the authors find that all six models fail the forecast-encompassing tests, indicating the potential for model improvement. The authors conclude that "the predictive performance of these models has implications for econometric practice, trade modeling, and the role of these models in policy making." One could argue that such conclusion supports Diehold's discussion as reviewed here.

Harvey, Leybourne, and Newbold (1998) discuss the fact that the forecast encompassing tests discussed previously are not robust to nonnormality in the forecast errors. They discuss several alternatives that are robust. For illustration, they consider the case in which the regression errors of the two competing models are generated by the bivariate Student's t-distribution of Dunnett and Sobel (1954), whose marginals are univariate Student's t-distributions (up to a multiplicative constant). They propose four alternative robust tests and use MC simulations to compare the estimated sizes to the nominal ones. They find that the four robust tests have approximately correct sizes in large samples, in sharp contrast with the nonrobust test. One of the four tests is a modified Diebold-Mariano (1995) test. The authors conclude: "We found that the Diebold-Mariano approach generates tests with good size and fairly good power properties, and we recommend that this approach be adopted."

3.2 Chong and Hendry (1986)

For presentation, we adopt a nonlinear extension of CH equations (4) and (5). The two contending single equation reduced form models are defined as

$$M_1(\alpha): y_t = g(x_t;\alpha) + u_{1t} \tag{3.1}$$

$$M_2(\delta): y_t = h(z_t;\delta) + u_{2t}, \quad t: 1 \to T+n. \tag{3.2}$$

The available sample is divided in two parts: (1) observations $t \in [1, T]$ are used to compute consistent estimates of α and δ (say, $\hat{\alpha}$ and $\hat{\delta}$); (2) observations $t \in [T+1, T+n]$ are then used to estimate the composite artificial model:

$$y_t = a_1 g(x_t;\hat{\alpha}) + a_2 h(z_t,\hat{\delta}) + v_t, \quad t: T+1 \to T+n, \tag{3.3}$$

where (a_1, a_2) are estimated by unconstrained OLS. Noting that the sampling variances of $(\hat{\alpha}, \hat{\delta})$ are generally of order $O(T^{-1})$ and might not be available for complex dynamic models, the CH test is run conditionally on $(\hat{\alpha}, \hat{\delta})$ and consists of testing the null hypothesis that $(a_1, a_2) = (1, 0)$. Actually, the authors note that "the *need* to pool forecasts is *prima facie* evidence of M_1 failure to encompass M_2." The nonlinear dependence of the CH-test on the M_1 and M_2 estimates $(\hat{\alpha}, \hat{\delta})$ and its HMR and DGM plims are illustrated next, using the linear example analyzed in section 2.9.

3.2.1 Example 2.9.1 (Continued)

The available sample is divided into

$$(y, W, X, Z) \in R^{N \times q} \tag{3.4}$$

$$(y_f, W_f, X_f, Z_f) \in R^{r \times q}, \tag{3.5}$$

with $q=1+p+k+l$. As before, eventual linear relationships between the exogenous variables are handled by using generalized inverses and degrees of freedom corrections. The OLS estimators, finite sample binding functions and pseudo-true values are defined in equations (2.43) to (2.45). The pooled forecasts are given by

$$\bar{y}_f = a_1 X_f \hat{\alpha} + a_2 Z_f \hat{\delta} + v_f. \tag{3.6}$$

The OLS estimator of (a_1, a_2) is

$$\begin{pmatrix} \hat{a}_1 \\ \hat{a}_2 \end{pmatrix} = \begin{pmatrix} \hat{\alpha}' X_f' X_f \hat{\alpha} & \hat{\alpha}' X_f' Z_f \hat{\delta} \\ \hat{\delta}' Z_f' X_f \hat{\alpha} & \hat{\delta}' Z_f' Z_f \hat{\delta} \end{pmatrix}^{-1} \begin{pmatrix} \hat{\alpha}' X_f' \\ \hat{\delta}' Z_f' \end{pmatrix} y_f. \tag{3.7}$$

Conditional on $M_1(\alpha)$, we have

$$\hat{\alpha} \to \alpha \text{ and } \hat{\delta} \to \delta_1(\alpha) = (Z'Z)^{-1} Z' X \alpha =_{say} P\alpha. \tag{3.8}$$

Therefore,

$$\begin{pmatrix} \hat{a}_1 \\ \hat{a}_2 \end{pmatrix} \xrightarrow[M_1(\alpha)]{} \begin{pmatrix} \alpha' X_f' X_f \alpha & \alpha' X_f' Z_f P\alpha \\ \alpha' P' Z_f' X_f \alpha & \alpha' P' Z_f' Z_f P\alpha \end{pmatrix}^{-1} \begin{pmatrix} \alpha' X_f' \\ \alpha' P' Z_f' \end{pmatrix} X_f \alpha = \begin{pmatrix} 1 \\ 0 \end{pmatrix}. \tag{3.9}$$

which confirms that the CH forecast encompassing test is indeed a test of H_0^{HMR}.

However, under $M_0(\theta)$, we have

$$\hat{\alpha} \to \alpha_0(\theta) = (X'X)^{-1} X' W \theta =_{say} R\theta \tag{3.10}$$

$$\hat{\delta} \to \delta_0(\theta) = (Z'Z)^{-1} Z' W \theta =_{say} S\theta, \tag{3.11}$$

and it follows that $(\hat{a}_1, \hat{a}_2)$ will not converge to (1, 0) unless $M_1(\alpha) \equiv M_0(\theta)$. Note that equation (3.7) treats symmetrically $M_1(\alpha)$ and $M_2(\delta)$ and also could be used to test whether M_2 encompasses M_1.

3.3 Forecast Encompassing

There exists a vast body of theoretical literature relative to tests of the predictive performances of competing models. See, for instance, Giacomini and White (2006) for an in-depth theoretical analysis of out-of-sample predictive tests and for an extensive list of related references. See also Inoue and Kilian (2006) on the selection of forecasting models and Shao (1993) and Racine (2000) on the use of cross-validation to select the model with the best predictive ability.

We do not intend to contribute here to that line of research. Instead, we propose to use forecast encompassing on carefully selected subsets of observations as a complement to, instead of a substitute for, encompassing. Especially with dynamic macro models, it is frequently the case that the data is nonstationary (e.g., unit root) and/or exhibits structural shocks (e.g., recessions). If one's preferred model $M_1(\hat{\alpha})$ failed to properly account for such problems, it would likely fail to encompass alternative $M_2(\hat{\delta})$ models, such as more flexible univariate dynamic equations. In such cases, one would want to identify eventual causes of such rejection. But even if $M_1(\hat{\alpha})$ did encompass $M_2(\hat{\delta})$, we might also explore whether $M_1(\hat{\alpha})$ could be improved further. In both cases, we argue that forecast encompassing of carefully selected subsets of observations could provide an important tool for identifying those observations that are most influential for encompassing, or the lack thereof.

Since forecast encompassing is meant to be a complement to encompassing, we only consider its section 2.5 version which, as briefly discussed here, is much easier to implement than its eventual HMR version. The forecast encompassing procedure that we propose is based upon the generalized version of encompassing introduced in section 2.10. Operational simulated versions thereof will be presented in chapter 5. Specifically, the M_2-forecast errors associated with equation (3.2) and to be tentatively encompassed by $M_1(\hat{\alpha})$ are given by

$$\hat{e}_t = y_t - h(z_t; \hat{\delta}), \quad t \in T_f \tag{3.12}$$

and are indeed functions of $\hat{\delta}$ and y_t. Obviously, equation (3.12) applies to cross-sectional as well as time-series data. Therefore, t is used as a generic index for individual observations, and T_f denotes the selected forecast interval.

We shall not introduce an explicit notation to distinguish the "forecast" period from the "estimation" period since such a distinction will generally be context dependent. If, in particular, forecast encompassing is to be used to gain additional insights into the eventual sources of $M_1(\hat{\alpha})$ failures to encompass M_2, it could be the case that the forecast periods under investigation would be subsets of the estimation period, regrouping, for example, those observations that would be thought to be most influential in such context. An application to the nonlinear model 2.9.2 is presented next.

The application of encompassing to the M_2 forecast errors in equation (3.12) is conceptually straightforward for $M_1(\alpha)$ and $M_2(\delta)$, as defined in equations (3.1) and (3.2), respectively. The $M_1(\hat{\alpha})$ expectations of the M_2-forecast errors in equation (3.12) are given by

$$\mathbb{E}(\hat{e}_t | M_1(\hat{\alpha})) = g(x_t; \hat{\alpha}) - d_1(x_t, z_t; \hat{\alpha}), \quad t \in T_f, \tag{3.13}$$

where

$$d_1(x_t, z_t; \hat{\alpha}) = \mathbb{E}[h(z_t; \hat{\delta}) | M_1(\hat{\alpha})], \quad t \in T_f. \tag{3.14}$$

The corresponding M_2-forecast encompassing differences are given by

$$\hat{\phi}_t = \hat{e}_t - \mathbb{E}[\hat{e}_t | M_1(\hat{\alpha})] \tag{3.15}$$

$$= [y_t - g(x_t; \hat{\alpha})] - [h(z_t; \hat{\delta}) - d_1(x_t, z_t; \hat{\alpha})], \quad t \in T_f. \tag{3.16}$$

This decomposition is particularly useful for the interpretation of the results since the first factor in equation (3.16) represents the $M_1(\hat{\alpha})$-forecast error, while the second term represents the difference between the $M_2(\hat{\delta})$ prediction and its expectation under $M_1(\hat{\alpha})$.

It would be unusual to compute t-statistics for individual forecast errors, except possibly in the case of an obvious outlier. More generally, one might prefer computing aggregate χ^2 statistics for selected subsets of observations. Let $\hat{e}_f$ and $\hat{\phi}_f$ denote p-dimensional vectors consisting of $\{\hat{e}_t : t \in T_f\}$ and $\{\hat{\phi}_t : t \in T_f\}$, respectively. As discussed in section 2.6, a χ^2-statistic for $\hat{e}_f$ requires computing the conditional covariance matrix

$$\hat{V}_f = \text{Var}(\hat{e}_f | M_1(\hat{\alpha})). \tag{3.17}$$

Most important, the evaluation of $\hat{V}_f$ only requires computing $d_1(x_t, z_t; \hat{\alpha})$ once for each $\hat{e}_t$, $t \in T_f$ since $\hat{\alpha}$ is kept fixed. The χ^2 statistic for $\hat{e}_f$ is given by

$$\hat{\phi}_f' \hat{V}_f^{-1} \hat{\phi}_f \xrightarrow[M_1(\hat{\alpha})]{} \chi^2(p). \tag{3.18}$$

For $p = 1$, the corresponding t-statistic for that individual M_2-forecast error obtains as the signed square root of $\chi^2(1)$.

We note that forecast encompassing is inherently a partial concept since it applies to a specific subset of observations, while encompassing relies upon the complete sample. It follows that forecast encompassing is neither necessary nor sufficient for encompassing. In particular, it could be the case that $M_1(\hat{\alpha})$ encompasses $M_2(\hat{\delta})$ and, nevertheless, fails to forecast encompass $M_2(\hat{\delta})$ for some specific subsample. Such circumstances could provide useful clues for eventual further improvements of $M_1(\hat{\alpha})$.

3.3.1 Example 2.9.1 (Continued)

Let models $M_1(\hat{\alpha})$ and $M_2(\hat{\delta})$ be the linear models described by equations (2.41) and (2.42), respectively. Let S_f denote the $r \times T$ selection matrix that maps (y, X, Z) into (y_f, X_f, Z_f); that is,

$$y_f = S_f y, \quad X_f = S_f X, \quad Z_f = S_f Z. \tag{3.19}$$

The expected values of y_f under $M_1(\hat{\alpha})$ and $M_2(\hat{\delta})$ are given by

$$g(X_f; \hat{\alpha}) = S_f X \hat{\alpha}, \quad \text{and} \tag{3.20}$$

$$h(Z_f;\hat{\delta}) = S_f Z\hat{\delta}, \tag{3.21}$$

respectively. The r-dimensional vector of $M_2(\hat{\delta})$ forecast errors to be encompassed is

$$\hat{e}_f = y_f - Z_f\hat{\delta} = S_f M_Z y. \tag{3.22}$$

Its expectation and covariance matrix conditional on $M_1(\hat{\alpha})$ are given by

$$\mathbb{E}(\hat{e}_f | M_1(\hat{\alpha})) = S_f M_Z X\hat{\alpha}, \text{ and} \tag{3.23}$$

$$\hat{V}_f = \text{Var}(\hat{e}_f | M_1(\hat{\alpha})) = \sigma^2 S_f M_Z S_f', \tag{3.24}$$

respectively. The corresponding forecast encompassing difference and χ^2 statistics are

$$\hat{\phi}_f = \hat{e}_f - \mathbb{E}(\hat{e}_f | M_1(\hat{\alpha})) = S_f M_Z M_X y, \text{ and} \tag{3.25}$$

$$\hat{\phi}_f' \hat{V}_f^+ \hat{\phi}_f = \frac{1}{\sigma^2} y' M_X M_Z S_f' (S_f' M_Z S_f)^+ S_f M_Z M_X y \underset{M_1(\hat{\alpha})}{\longrightarrow} \chi^2(d), \tag{3.26}$$

respectively, where $(S_f' M_Z S_f)^+$ denotes the generalized inverse of $S_f' M_Z S_f$ and $d \leq p$ its rank.

As mentioned in section 3.2, forecast encompassing is neither necessary nor sufficient for encompassing. To illustrate this important distinction, consider the case where $M_X Z = 0$ which, as shown in example 2.9.1, implies that the overall encompassing difference in equation (2.55) is identically zero, and therefore that $M_1(\hat{\alpha})$ encompasses $\hat{\delta}$. It also implies that

$$M_Z M_X M_Z = M_Z M_X = M_X, \tag{3.27}$$

but it does not imply that the forecast encompassing difference $\hat{\phi}_f$ in equation (3.25) is zero. Instead, it simplifies as

$$\hat{\phi}_f = S_f M_X y = S_f(y - X\hat{\alpha}), \tag{3.28}$$

which is actually a selection of $M_1(\hat{\alpha})$ forecast errors. The χ^2 forecast encompassing statistic in equation (3.26) simplifies to

$$\hat{\phi}_f' \hat{V}_f^{-1} \hat{\phi}_f = \frac{1}{\sigma^2} y' M_X S_f' (S_f' M_Z S_f)^+ S_f M_X y \underset{M_1(\hat{\alpha})}{\longrightarrow} \chi^2(d), \tag{3.29}$$

which could still be significantly different from zero for some subsets of the $M_1(\hat{\alpha})$ forecast errors. Note that this χ^2 test statistic differs from the standard χ^2 test statistic, in that the middle matrix is $S_f' M_Z S_f$ instead of $S_f' M_X S_f$.

3.3.2 Example 2.9.2 (Continued)

We now apply both CH and forecast encompassing tests to the nonlinear example 2.9.2, referring to appendix 2B for notation and appendix 3A for additional

Table 3.1
Forecasts encompassing results (example 2.9.2)

Encompassing			Forecast Encompassing					
			CH High x				Equation (3.26)	
p_0	q_0	tst($\hat{\delta}\|\hat{\alpha}$)	$\hat{a}_1$	std($\hat{a}_1$)	$\hat{a}_2$	std ($\hat{a}_2$)	High x	Low x
0.75	0.75	0.247	1.122	0.1219	−0.0208	0.0619	232.1	291.3*
0.75	0.80	−0.539	0.9942	0.1093	−0.0283	0.0628	221.5	361.7*
0.75	0.85	−1.363	0.8744	0.0981	−0.0379	0.0641	222.8	490.9*
0.75	0.90	−2.240*	0.7589*	0.0884	−0.0507	0.0663	259.7	752.1*
0.75	0.95	−3.263*	0.6382*	0.0810	−0.0675	0.0710	497.3*	1,418*
0.95	0.95	0.505	1.013	0.0718	0.0128	0.0574	250.2	250.4
0.95	0.90	3.983*	1.163	0.0831	0.0737	0.0548	296.9*	202.2
0.95	0.85	6.598*	1.318*	0.0961	0.1097	0.0539	369.4*	215.8
0.95	0.80	8.786*	1.485*	0.1105	0.1339*	0.0535	447.6*	240.4
0.95	0.75	10.71*	1.668*	0.1262	0.1514*	0.0533	530.4*	267.2

Note: In columns 8 and 9, the 0.95 critical values for a $\chi^2(250) = 287.9$
*denotes test results exceeding the 0.95 critical value.

derivations. Specifically, we apply these tests to selected subsets of the 1,000 observations to highlight how they could be used in more complex empirical applications and to identify eventual sources of encompassing failures. With regard to example 2.9.2, we are dealing with three key factors:

1. The differences between the conditional expectations $\theta p_i x_i$ under $M_0(\theta)$, $\alpha q_i x_i$ under $M_1(\alpha)$, and δx_i under $M_2(\delta)$ are increasing in x_i.
2. The conditional variance of y_i given $M_1(\hat{\alpha})$, as shown in formula (3.A.6) is also increasing in x_i.
3. When $p_0 < q_0$, there is more censoring under the unknown DGP $M_0(\theta)$ than under $M_1(\alpha)$ and the converse is true as well. It follows that it might not be a priori obvious which subsets of observations best account for eventual $M_1(\hat{\alpha})$ failures to encompass $\hat{\delta}$. Therefore, we consider two opposite scenarios:
   a. A "low x" scenario, regrouping the 250 observations (1/4 of the samples) with the lowest x values.
   b. A "high x" scenario, regrouping the 250 observations with the highest x values.

- **CH forecast encompassing**: The application of the CH test to both scenarios is straightforward. It only requires computing the conditional expectations of y_i for $i \in I_f$ under $M_1(\hat{\alpha})$ and $M_2(\hat{\delta})$:

$$\hat{y}_{i,1} = \hat{\alpha} q_i x_i, \qquad \hat{y}_{i,2} = \hat{\delta} x_i, \qquad i \in I_f, \tag{3.30}$$

respectively, and regressing $\{y_i\}$ on $\{\hat{y}_{i,1}, \hat{y}_{2,i}\}$ without an intercept. The CH results for the "high x" (250 observations) scenario are reported in columns 4 to 7 of table 3.1 and are in overall agreement with the earlier encompassing results reproduced in column 3 (for the full sample of 1,000 observations). In sharp contrast, the results for the CH "low x" scenario, which are not reported in table 3.1, are useless due to a very high correlation between $\{\hat{y}_{i,1}\}$ and $\{\hat{y}_{i,2}\}$ for that scenario, which produces meaningless large positive and negative values for $(\hat{a}_1, \hat{a}_2)$, together with equally large least squares standard deviations. Therefore, it is obvious that it is the "high x" scenario that is most influential, according to the CH test.

- **Forecast encompassing**: The application of the forecast encompassing test requires deriving the joint distribution of the relevant M_2 forecast errors under $M_1(\hat{\alpha})$. These are given by

$$\hat{e}_i = y_i - \hat{\delta} x_i, \quad i \in I_f. \tag{3.31}$$

It is important to note that while forecast encompassing is restricted to a specific subset of observations $i \in I_f$, the underlying distributions of y_i and $\hat{\delta}$ conditional on $M_1(\hat{\alpha})$ are based upon the entire sample. Therefore, in the formulas that follow, i and j are restricted to I_f, while the summation index k runs from 1 to N, covering the full sample.

The conditional expectation of $\hat{e}_i$ given $M_1(\hat{\alpha})$ equals

$$\mathbb{E}(\hat{e}_i | M_1(\hat{\alpha})) = \hat{\alpha} q_i x_i - \delta_1(\hat{\alpha}) x_i = (q_i - \gamma)\hat{\alpha} x_i, \quad i \in I_f, \tag{3.32}$$

where γ denotes the weighted sum of q_k values:

$$\gamma = \frac{\sum q_k x_k^2}{\sum x_k^2}, \quad k: 1 \to N. \tag{3.33}$$

As shown in appendix 3A, the conditional variances and covariances of the $\hat{e}_i$ values ($i \in I_f$) are given by

$$\mathrm{Var}(\hat{e}_i | M_1(\hat{\alpha})) = v_i^2(1 - 2x_i\phi_i) + x_i^2 \,\mathrm{Var}(\hat{\delta} | M_1(\hat{\alpha})), \quad i \in I_f \tag{3.34}$$

$$\mathrm{Cov}(\hat{e}_i, \hat{e}_j | M_1(\hat{\alpha})) = -(x_j\phi_i v_i^2 + x_i\phi_j v_j^2) + x_i x_j \,\mathrm{Var}(\hat{\delta} | M_1(\hat{\alpha})), \quad i \neq j \in I_f^2, \tag{3.35}$$

where

$$\phi_i = \frac{x_i}{\sum x_k^2}, \quad \mathrm{Var}(\hat{\delta} | M_1(\hat{\alpha})) = \sum \phi_k^2 v_k^2, \quad k: 1 \to N \tag{3.36}$$

$$v_i^2 = \mathrm{Var}(y_i|M_1(\hat{\alpha})) = \sigma^2 + q_i(1 - q_i)(\hat{\alpha}x_i)^2, \tag{3.37}$$

as defined in equations (2.B.6) and (2.B.7), respectively. The χ^2 forecast encompassing test statistic then obtains from equation (3.18).

The results are presented in columns 8 and 9 of table 3.1. Intriguingly, we note that the low x scenario is more effective when $q_0 > p_0$ (i.e., there is less censoring under $M_1(\hat{\alpha})$ than under the unknown DGP), while it is the high x scenario that is more effective in the opposite case. Obviously, in this very simple example, one does not need forecast encompassing to work out in which direction to adjust q_0 to address encompassing failures. Nor would it be difficult to add moment conditions to jointly estimate $\hat{\alpha}$ and q_0, relying upon the simulation techniques discussed in chapter 5. But, in any event, this simple example has shown that forecast encompassing provides flexible and operational complements to encompassing.

As a side comment, we note that, when p_0 is close to 1 and $q_0 < p_0$, under both encompassing and forecast encompassing (the high x scenario), $M_1(\hat{\alpha})$ quickly fails to encompass $M_2(\hat{\delta})$ as q_0 decreases. On the other hand, when $q_0 > p_0$, it appears that forecast encompassing (the low x scenario) is significantly more effective than both encompassing and CH high x forecast encompassing in detecting $M_1(\hat{\alpha})$ failures to encompass $M_2(\hat{\delta})$. This highlights the importance of being able to rely upon a variety of related encompassing approaches tailored to the empirical application under consideration.

3.4 Conclusions

In serious empirical applications, none of the analytical results derived for example 3.3.2 will ever be available. Nevertheless, as discussed in chapters 4 and 5, all the encompassing tests we presented in chapters 2 and 3 can easily be computed using MC simulations under the minimal requirement (for meaningful inference) that both $M_1(\hat{\alpha})$ and $M_2(\hat{\delta})$ be amenable to MC simulations.

In such cases, an eventual overall failure of $M_1(\hat{\alpha})$ to encompass $M_2(\hat{\delta})$ might not always be easy to interpret. As already discussed in section 2.3, this is a key reason to conduct an encompassing t-test for each individual component of $\hat{\delta}$. As we shall see for the timber auction application in chapter 6, this individual approach is indeed very informative in the search for an improved $M_1(\hat{\alpha})$. But these are also circumstances under which the application of forecast encompassing tests to carefully selected subsets of potentially influential or suspicious observations provides computationally cheap (under MC simulations) and effective complementary tools for identifying both the sources of eventual failures to encompass and/or ways to improve further the encompassing performance of $M_1(\hat{\alpha})$.

Appendix 3A: Derivations of Equations (3.34) and (3.35)

We rely upon the notation introduced in appendix 2B—namely, equations (2.B.1) to (2.B.7). For ease of notation, $M_1(\hat{\alpha})$ is denoted as $\hat{M}_1$. In this appendix we derive the covariance matrix of $\{\hat{e}_i, i \in I_f\}$ conditional on $\hat{M}_1$.

It follows from the definition of $\hat{e}_i$ in equation (3.31) that

$$\operatorname{Var}(\hat{e}_i|\hat{M}_1) = \operatorname{Var}(y_i|\hat{M}_1) - 2x_i \operatorname{Cov}(y_i, \hat{\delta}|\hat{M}_1) + x_i^2 \operatorname{Var}(\hat{\delta}|\hat{M}_1). \tag{3.A.1}$$

Using the results in appendix 2B, we find that

$$\operatorname{Var}(y_i|\hat{M}_1) = v_i^2 = \sigma^2 + q_i(1-q_i)(\hat{\alpha}x_i)^2. \tag{3.A.2}$$

Furthermore, since $\hat{\delta} = \sum_k \phi_k y_k$, we also have

$$\operatorname{Cov}(y_i, \hat{\delta}|\hat{M}_1) = \phi_i v_i^2 \tag{3.A.3}$$

$$\operatorname{Var}(\hat{\delta}|\hat{M}_1) = \sum_k \phi_k^2 v_k^2. \tag{3.A.4}$$

Therefore,

$$\operatorname{Var}(\hat{e}_i|\hat{M}_1) = v_i^2(1 - 2x_i\phi_i) + x_i^2 \operatorname{Var}(\hat{\delta}|\hat{M}_1). \tag{3.A.5}$$

Similarly,

$$\begin{aligned} \operatorname{Cov}(\hat{e}_i\hat{e}_j|\hat{M}_1) &= \operatorname{Cov}(y_iy_j|\hat{M}_1) - x_i \operatorname{Cov}(y_j, \hat{\delta}|\hat{M}_1) \\ &\quad - x_j \operatorname{Cov}(y_i, \hat{\delta}|\hat{M}_1) + x_ix_j \operatorname{Var}(\hat{\delta}|\hat{M}_1) \\ &= -(x_i\phi_j v_j^2 + x_j\phi_i v_i^2) + x_ix_j \operatorname{Var}(\hat{\delta}|\hat{M}_1). \end{aligned} \tag{3.A.6}$$

4

Method of Simulated Moments (MSM)

This chapter is organized as follows: section 4.1 presents an introduction to the development of simulation methods in econometrics. MSM estimation is introduced in section 4.2. The selection of the moments and weight matrix is discussed in section 4.3. The finite sample distribution of MSM estimators is derived in section 4.4. Section 4.5 applies MSM to example 2.9.2. Finally, section 4.6 offers a short literature review of MSM and related concepts.

4.1 Introduction

An excellent introduction to the development of simulation-based econometric methods is offered by Gouriéroux and Monfort (1996, section 1.1), where the authors distinguish three main periods in the postwar history of econometric methods:

1. Before 1960, progress was made mainly in terms of models whose estimators had analytical expressions, such as models from the exponential family of distributions for which analytical ML estimators were available.
2. The 1970s and 1980s saw the development of numerical optimization algorithms. It became possible to compute estimators that lacked analytical expressions, such as ML. That period also saw the introduction of alternative criterion functions, leading to the development of a broad class of GMM estimators.
3. Starting in the 1990s, the development of MC simulation techniques in econometrics allowed the computation of criterion functions depending on high-dimensional integrals lacking analytical solutions. This difficulty could now be circumvented by MC simulations, leading to the development of MSM to be defined in section 4.2.

In parallel to these impressive theoretical and computational advances, the last 25 years have witnessed an equally dramatic expansion of the volume as well as the quality of available economic data. The combination of those two factors has enabled practitioners to develop and estimate increasingly sophisticated empirical applications. Unsurprisingly, these models are often estimated by MSM since, as we shall discuss further in section 4.2, the only requirement is that the models under consideration be amenable to MC simulations which, in our view, is a minimal requirement for meaningful statistical inference.

An additional important benefit of MC simulation of a tentative model is that watching a model in action can provide useful guidance as to the model's capability to replicate key features of the data or, under encompassing, findings from a rival model, as well as guidance for further extensions of one's model.

Beyond the fact that likelihood-based inference is generally both analytically and numerically intractable for most policy-oriented empirical models, there is an issue of a fundamental trade-off between statistical efficiency and robustness against specification errors. In particular, ML estimators are theoretically efficient (as they use all the information contained in the likelihood specification), but this property requires an axiom of "correct specification" that is clearly unattainable in practice. It follows that ML estimators will generally be less robust against unavoidable specification errors than less efficient alternatives, such as MSM.

Given that DGPs are unattainable, empirical models thereof will be inherently misspecified. This is where the encompassing of alternative models ought to play a key role in the validation of one's preferred model as a sound basis for policy analysis. However, since current concepts of encompassing, as reviewed in section 2.2, are likelihood-based, it is essential to develop broadly applicable, simulation-based versions of encompassing that rely on MSM to the effect that they will require only that the models under consideration be amenable to MC simulations.

Last but not least, there have been major advances in the development of numerically efficient MC simulation techniques, whose main objective is that of reducing the MC sampling variance inherent to any brute force simulation. The only such technique used in section 4.5 and for the timber auction application in chapter 6 is that known as common random numbers (CRNs), whereby successive MC replications are initialized with a common seed to smooth the MSM objective function. As discussed, for example, in Hendry (1995, section 3.6), there is a variety of "variance reduction" techniques that can be used to increase the numerical efficiency of MC simulation techniques. How to eventually implement them for MSM and encompassing is a topic left for future investigations.

On the other hand, recent developments in parallel or distributed computing should considerably accelerate the computation of simulation-based encompassing statistics since, as we shall see, the required simulations are "embarrassingly parallel," in the terminology of computer experts. This concept will not be discussed further in this book, but the potential for such major reductions in computing time will be obvious from our presentation of simulation encompassing in chapter 5.

4.2 MSM Estimation (Inner Loop)

A textbook presentation of MSM can be found in Davidson and MacKinnon (2004, section 9.6). Additional references will be provided in section 4.6.

Let $M_1(\alpha)$ denote a parametric model of interest with $\alpha \in R^k$. Let $Y \in R^{N \times p}$ denote a sample of size N, with p denoting the number of endogenous observable variables. Obviously, there are also exogenous variables $X \in R^{N \times r}$, but they are omitted for the ease of notation.

1. The first and critical step in implementing MSM consists of selecting a vector of "sample moments," such as $\hat{m}(Y) \in R^l$ with $l > k$. These are meant to characterize key sample features of model $M_1(\alpha)$. Ultimately, the estimation of $M_1(\alpha)$ will rely exclusively on these specific moments, whose selection is discussed in section 4.3.1.
2. An MSM estimate of α obtains by numerical minimization of the quadratic objective function:

$$f(\alpha) = [\hat{m}(Y) - \bar{m}(\alpha)]' \hat{W}^{-1} [\hat{m}(Y) - \bar{m}(\alpha)], \tag{4.1}$$

where $\bar{m}(\alpha)$ denotes an MC estimate of the expectation of $\hat{m}(Y)$ given $M_1(\alpha)$:

$$\bar{m}(\alpha) = \mathbb{E}[\hat{m}(Y)|M_1(\alpha)] \tag{4.2}$$

and $\hat{W}$ denotes a $l \times l$ positive definite weight matrix, whose choice is discussed in section 4.3.2.

The MSM estimate of α, such as $\hat{\alpha}_{MSM}$, obtains by numerical minimization of $f(\alpha)$:

$$\hat{\alpha}_{MSM} = \operatorname{argmin} f(\alpha). \tag{4.3}$$

Note: A more general version of MSM allows for moment conditions or observation functions that are functions of both Y and α, such as $\hat{m}(Y;\alpha)$. See, for instance, Duffie and Singleton (1993, equation (3.2)). In such a case, $\bar{m}(\alpha)$ in equation (4.2) would be replaced by

$$\bar{m}(\alpha) = \mathbb{E}[\hat{m}(Y;\alpha)|M_1(\alpha)], \tag{4.4}$$

but equations (4.1) and (4.3) would be unchanged. For ease of notation, we will keep referring to the simpler case in equation (4.2), which is also the one used for the timber auction application in chapter 6. The MSM and simulation encompassing algorithms described next and in chapter 5 apply to both versions of $\bar{m}(\alpha)$.

There are also cases where $\hat{m}(Y;\alpha)$ is such that its expectation under $M_1(\alpha)$ is zero. In such a case, $\bar{m}(\alpha) = 0$. See, for example, Hansen (1982, assumption 2.4). The difference $\hat{m}(Y) - \bar{m}(\alpha)$ in equation (4.1) is then replaced by $\hat{m}(Y;\alpha)$, to the effect that MC simulations are not needed and the minimization of $f(\alpha)$ in equation (4.3) is obtained by GMM. See section 4.6.1 for references on this topic.

3. $\bar{m}(\alpha)$ obtains from an inner loop of S_1 MC draws of $\hat{m}(Y)$ given $M_1(\alpha)$, such as $\hat{m}(\tilde{Y}_i|\alpha), i: 1 \to S_1$. Specifically, draw i obtains as

$$M_1(\alpha) \to \tilde{Y}_i|\alpha \to \hat{m}(\tilde{Y}_i|\alpha), \qquad i: 1 \to S_1, \tag{4.5}$$

from which $\bar{m}(\alpha)$ is computed as

$$\bar{m}(\alpha) = \frac{1}{S_1} \sum_{i=1}^{S_1} \hat{m}(\tilde{Y}_i|\alpha). \tag{4.6}$$

We note that parallel or distributed computing of $\{\hat{m}|\tilde{Y}_i(\alpha)\}$ would produce large reductions in computing time. As discussed previously, it is important that the sequence of $\tilde{Y}_i$ draws for different values of α be initialized by a common seed in order to smooth the objective function $f(\alpha)$; this technique, known as that of CRNs, was briefly mentioned in section 4.1.

4. To minimize the objective function $f(\alpha)$ in equation (4.1), we recommend using a simplex optimizer (such as the subroutine DUMPOL in the IMSL FORTRAN library) since it requires no analytical nor numerical gradients and/or Hessian matrices, just a function subroutine for $f(\alpha)$, plus standard auxiliary inputs such as initial values, scale factors, and convergence criteria. To avoid nuisance corner solutions, exact restrictions on α should be handled by appropriate transformations of unconstrained auxiliary parameters. Consider, for example, an individual coefficient $\alpha_j > 0$ that can be reparameterized as

$$\alpha_j = \alpha_{j0} \exp \beta_j, \text{ with } \beta_j \in R, \tag{4.7}$$

where α_{j0} denotes a fixed initial value. Other examples of such auxiliary reparameterization will be presented for the timber auction application in appendix 6A.

4.3 Selection of the Moments and Weight Matrix

4.3.1 The Moments $\hat{m}(Y)$

The first and most critical step in implementing MSM consists of selecting a vector of sample moments $\hat{m}(Y) \in R^l$, with $l > k$. These are meant to characterize key sample features of the model under consideration. This is critical since, ultimately, the estimation and interpretation of $M_1(\hat{\alpha})$ will rely exclusively on its capability to account for these specific moments. Therefore, to obtain meaningful (i.e., policy-relevant) results, it is essential to prioritize those aspects of the data that are most relevant for the intended use of the model.

Relatedly, selecting l to be too close to k would likely result in an excellent but spurious fit. Conversely, when l is much larger than k, there is an obvious risk of diluting the most relevant moment information within an excess of nuisance information.

Surprisingly, while MSM is increasingly used in serious empirical applications, we found limited discussion of the frequently ad hoc selection of moments, with a wide range of l values, from $l = k$ (perfect fit) to l much larger (1,000+) than k. An early theoretical but relevant discussion of "which moments to match" (in the context of GMM) can be found in Gallant and Tauchen (1996): "We present a systematic approach to generating moment conditions for the generalized method of moments (GMM) estimator (Hansen, 1982) of the parameters of a structural model. The approach is an alternative to the common practice of selecting a few low-order moments on an ad hoc basis and then proceeding with GMM. The idea is simple: Use the expectation under the structural model of the score from an auxiliary model as the vector of moments conditions." While the authors' analysis is fairly technical, it also applies to MSM and provides intuition and support for the moment selection procedure presented next.

Specifically, we propose to use as moments the least squares estimators of a seemingly unrelated regression equations (SURE) system of linear equations for the dependent variables most likely to be affected by the situation under scrutiny.

The regressors are then selected as the exogenous (or lagged endogenous) variables that best account for the observed variations of the dependent variables across observations. Assuming a SURE system of p equations on q common regressors, unconstrained OLS estimation provides a total of $l = p \cdot q$ "moment" conditions (and constrained estimation can also be used to eliminate insignificant coefficients).

For example, for the timber auction data presented in chapter 6, we observe what appears to be suspiciously low prices and low numbers of registered bidders, two key observations suggestive of potential collusion. Hence, we selected as sample moments the coefficients of a two-equation SURE system for the logarithms of price and number of bidders as functions of q auction specific covariates to achieve a total of $l = 2q > k$ sample moments.

Another illustration of the importance of selecting moments that are conditional on the exogenous variables is provided in section 4.5 (example 2.9.2 continued).

4.3.2 The Weight Matrix $\hat{W}$

The selection of $\hat{W}$ has been extensively discussed in the GMM and MSM literature reviewed in section 4.6. Consistency of $\hat{\alpha}_{MSM}$ requires only that $\hat{W}$ be positive definite. Conditional on $M_1(\alpha)$ being correctly specified, an optimal choice for asymptotic efficiency—within the class of MSM estimators associated with the objective function $f(\alpha)$—would be one where $\hat{W}$ converges to the covariance matrix of $\hat{m}(Y)$ given $M_1(\alpha)$. There are two main reasons for not considering that theoretical approach in the present context:

1. *Computational*: It requires computationally intensive MSM iterations until a fixed point solution obtains for $\hat{\alpha}_{MSM}$ and $\hat{W}$.
2. *Theoretical*: These efficiency results are conditional on $M_1(\alpha)$ being correctly specified. As discussed in chapter 1, this is not a realistic assumption in serious empirical applications.

Actually, the SURE selection of moments discussed here also produces an obvious choice for $\hat{W}$, specifically the covariance matrix of the SURE coefficients $\hat{m}(Y)$, which offers two key advantages:

1. It requires no iterations since it only depends on Y, not on α.
2. Foremost, the actual data Y was generated by the unknown DGP, not by $M_1(\alpha)$. It immediately follows that the SURE covariance matrix $\hat{W}$ is also implicitly generated by the DGP and therefore will converge to the asymptotic covariance matrix of $\hat{m}(Y)$ under the DGP.

The four steps required for the MSM estimation of $M_1(\alpha)$ are summarized in table 4.1.

4.4 Finite Sample Distribution of $\hat{\alpha}_{MSM}$ (Outer Loop)

Empirical applications such as that presented in chapter 6 are far too complicated to consider deriving asymptotic properties for the MSM estimator $\hat{\alpha}_{MSM}$. Instead, once $\hat{\alpha}_{MSM}$ obtains, we can rely upon an outer loop of auxiliary MC

Table 4.1
MSM estimation of $M_1(\alpha)$

1. Sample moments: $Y \to \hat{m}(Y)$ and $\hat{W}$.

2. "Inner loop" MC computation of $\bar{m}(\alpha)$ for any given α:

$$M_1(\alpha) \underset{MC}{\longrightarrow} \{\tilde{Y}_i \to \hat{m}(\tilde{Y}_i|\alpha)\}_{i=1}^{S_1}$$

$$\longrightarrow \bar{m}(\alpha) = \frac{1}{S_1}\sum_{i=1}^{S_1} \hat{m}(\tilde{Y}_i|\alpha).$$

3. Objective function:

$$f(\alpha) = [\hat{m}(Y) - \bar{m}(\alpha)]'\hat{W}^{-1}[\hat{m}(Y) - \bar{m}(\alpha)].$$

4. Optimization: $\hat{\alpha}_{MSM} = \text{argmin} f(\alpha)$.

Table 4.2
Finite sample distribution of $\hat{\alpha}_{MSM}$

1. "Outer loop" draws from $M_1(\hat{\alpha}_{MSM})$:

$$M_1(\hat{\alpha}_{MSM}) \to \{\tilde{Y}_j\}_{j=1}^{S_2}.$$

2. For each $\tilde{Y}_j$, replicate the MSM estimation of α, following steps 1 to 4 in table 4.1, specifically

$$\{\tilde{Y}_j\}_{j=1}^{S_2} \to \{\hat{\alpha}_{MSM,j}, f(\hat{\alpha}_{MSM,j}), \ldots\}_{j=1}^{S_2}.$$

3. Means, standard deviations, and t-statistics for individual $\hat{\alpha}$ coefficients and other statistics of interest.

simulations of $M_1(\hat{\alpha}_{MSM})$ to produce finite sample moments for $\hat{\alpha}_{MSM}$, as well as for any other statistic of interest related to $M_1(\hat{\alpha}_{MSM})$.

Specifically, we draw S_2 independent (MC) auxiliary datasets $\{\tilde{Y}_j\}_{j=1}^{S_2}$ from $M_1(\hat{\alpha}_{MSM})$ and, for each simulated dataset, replicate exactly (moments, initial values, ...) the MSM inner loop procedure described in table 4.1 to produce a set of S_2 independent simulated MSM estimates, such as $\{\tilde{\alpha}_{MSM,j}\}_{j=1}^{S_2}$, from which we can compute finite sample means, standard deviations, and t-statistics for the individual components of $\hat{\alpha}_{MSM}$, as well as for $f(\hat{\alpha}_{MSM})$ and any other statistic of interest in the context of $M_1(\alpha)$. These are essential for an eventual sequential specification search for a best model $M_1(\alpha)$ and, obviously, for the interpretation of key coefficients and/or statistics derived from these. See table 4.2 for a summary.

Table 4.3
GMM and MSM results (example 2.9.2)
$(S_1 = 50, S_2 = 40)$

			$\hat{\alpha}_{GMM}$			$\hat{\alpha}_{MSM}$	
p_0	q_0	$\hat{\alpha}_{GMM}$	Mean	Std	$\hat{\alpha}_{MSM}$	Mean	Std
0.75	0.75	0.3080	0.3075	0.0076	0.3079	0.3077	0.0075
0.75	0.80	0.2938	0.2927	0.0083	0.2941	0.2926	0.0083
0.75	0.85	0.2778	0.2775	0.0070	0.2776	0.2776	0.0071
0.75	0.90	0.2582	0.2558	0.0051	0.2573	0.2557	0.0052
0.75	0.95	0.2296	0.2292	0.0054	0.2290	0.2292	0.0054
0.95	0.95	0.3069	0.3007	0.0061	0.3000	0.3006	0.0063
0.95	0.90	0.3268	0.3273	0.0064	0.3267	0.3271	0.0067
0.95	0.85	0.3437	0.3434	0.0080	0.3437	0.3435	0.0080
0.95	0.80	0.3573	0.3575	0.0086	0.3576	0.3577	0.0088
0.95	0.75	0.3693	0.3671	0.0105	0.3672	0.3674	0.0108

In particular, we can trivially produce a t-statistic for $f(\tilde{\alpha}_{MSM})$ from the sequence $\{f(\tilde{\alpha}_{MSM,j})\}_{j=1}^{S_2}$. This is obviously a critical statistic to measure the inherent degree of misspecification (and/or overidentification) of $M_1(\hat{\alpha}_{MSM})$ and one that would be empirically far more relevant than an asymptotic (noncentral chi-squared) approximation thereof. The same method can be applied to $M_2(\hat{\delta}_{MSM})$ to produce M_2-sampling distribution for $\hat{\delta}_{MSM}$.

Note: Obviously, the simulation algorithm described in table 4.2 is not specific to MSM. It applies to any estimation procedure. Specifically, it would amount to replacing the MSM step 2 in table 4.2 by the alternative estimation procedure under consideration. This would be relevant for encompassing since the owner of the alternative model $M_2(\delta)$ might have used a different estimation procedure and, assuming that we get access to that procedure, we might not want to reprogram the estimation of $M_2(\delta)$.

4.5 Example 2.9.2 (continued)

We apply both GMM (actually OLS) and MSM to example 2.9.2 for a sample size $N = 1{,}000$ under the same parameter values $(\theta, \sigma, m, s) = (0.3, 0.1, 5, 3)$ as those used to produce table 2.1.

1. **GMM**: the conditional sample moment under consideration is given by

$$\hat{m}(y) = \sum_{i=1}^{N} q_i x_i y_i, \tag{4.8}$$

where division by N is omitted for the ease of notation. Its expectation under $M_1(\alpha)$ is given by

$$m(\alpha) = \alpha \sum_{i=1}^{N} q_i^2 x_i^2. \tag{4.9}$$

Therefore, minimization of

$$f(\alpha) = (\hat{m}(y) - m(\alpha))^2 \tag{4.10}$$

produces the GMM/OLS estimator $\hat{\alpha}$ in equation (2.67):

$$\hat{\alpha}_{GMM} = \sum_{i=1}^{N} \psi_i y_i, \text{ with } \psi_i = \frac{q_i x_i}{\sum_{i=1}^{N} q_i^2 x_i^2}. \tag{4.11}$$

Its analytical sampling variance obtains from equations (2.B.1) and (2.B.6) in appendix 2B:

$$\text{Var}(\hat{\alpha}_{GMM}) = \sum_{i=1}^{N} \psi_i^2 v_i^2, \text{ where} \tag{4.12}$$

v_i^2 denotes $\text{Var}(y_i|M_1(\hat{\alpha}_{MSM}))$.

2. **MSM**: as described in table 4.1, MSM estimation of $\bar{m}(\alpha)$ for any given value of α (as selected by the optimizer) requires an inner loop of S_1 MC simulations of $M_1(\alpha)$. Steps 2 and 3 in table 4.1 proceed as follows:

   - Step 2 (inner loop for any given α)

$$\alpha \to \tilde{y}_{i,j} = \begin{cases} \tilde{u}_{i,j} & \text{proba } 1 - q_i \\ \alpha x_i + \tilde{u}_{i,j} & \text{proba } q_i, \end{cases} \tag{4.13}$$

   where $\tilde{u}_{i,j} \sim IN(0, \sigma^2)$, for $i: 1 \to N$ and $j: 1 \to S_2$. Therefore,

$$\tilde{m}_j = \sum_{i=1}^{N} q_i x_i \tilde{y}_{i,j}, \qquad \text{and } \bar{m}(\alpha) = \frac{1}{S_1} \sum_{j=1}^{S_1} \tilde{m}_j. \tag{4.14}$$

   - Step 3 (objective function):

$$f(\alpha) = (\sum_{i=1}^{N} q_i x_i y_i - \bar{m}(\alpha))^2. \tag{4.15}$$

   - Step 4 (minimization):

$$\hat{\alpha}_{MSM} = \text{argmin} f(\alpha). \tag{4.16}$$

The GMM (OLS) and MSM estimates of α are reported in columns 3 and 6 of table 4.3 for the 10 cases considered in table 2.1. The MSM estimates rely on an inner loop of $S_1 = 50$ MC simulations. The GMM results in table 4.3 differ slightly from the OLS results in table 2.1 due to the use of a different random seed.

3. The MC standard deviations of the GMM and MSM estimates (treating σ^2 as known) obtain as described in table 4.2 using an outer loop of $S_2 = 40$ samples drawn from $M_1(\hat{\alpha}_{GMM})$ and $M_1(\hat{\alpha}_{MSM})$, respectively. In table 4.3, which has eight columns, the results are reported in columns (4,5) for the GMM results, and in columns (7,8) for the MSM results.

   As expected, we find that the GMM (OLS) and MSM results are very close to one another due to a combination of large sample size ($N = 1{,}000$), small σ ($\sigma = 0.1$), similar objective functions, and the use of a common set of simulated random draws for the u_i values used for both $\hat{\alpha}_{GMM}$ and $\hat{\alpha}_{MSM}$ MC simulations.

4. In section 4.3.1, we discussed the importance of selecting conditional sample moments that are most relevant for the estimation of α. To illustrate this critical point, note first that the OLS estimator in equation (2.67) can be reinterpreted as the GMM estimator associated with the *conditional* moment condition[1]

$$\hat{m}(y) = \sum q_i x_i y_i, \tag{4.17}$$

ignoring the $1/N$ factor for ease of notation. Its conditional expectation under $M_1(\alpha)$ is given by

$$\bar{m}(\alpha) = \alpha \sum q_i^2 x_i^2. \tag{4.18}$$

The corresponding GMM estimator is

$$\hat{\alpha}_{GMM} = \frac{\sum q_i x_i y_i}{\sum q_i^2 x_i^2} = \hat{\alpha}, \tag{4.19}$$

as expected. Suppose that instead, we had selected the unconditional moment

$$\hat{m}(y) = \sum y_i, \text{ for which} \tag{4.20}$$

$$\bar{m}(\alpha) = \alpha \sum q_i x_i, \text{ and} \tag{4.21}$$

$$\hat{\alpha}_{GMM} = \frac{\sum y_i}{\sum q_i x_i}. \tag{4.22}$$

Obviously, this alternative GMM estimator remains consistent. If, however, we apply the same moment condition to $M_2(\delta)$, we find that

$$\hat{\delta}_{GMM} = \frac{\sum y_i}{\sum x_i}, \text{ and} \tag{4.23}$$

$$\delta_1(\alpha) = \alpha \frac{\sum q_i x_i}{\sum x_i}. \tag{4.24}$$

It immediately follows from equations (4.22) and (4.24) that

$$\delta_1(\hat{\alpha}_{GMM}) = \frac{\sum y_i}{\sum x_i} = \hat{\delta}, \tag{4.25}$$

leading to the erroneous conclusion that $M_1(\hat{\alpha}_{GMM})$ encompasses $M_2(\hat{\delta}_{GMM})$, regardless of the q_i values. This univariate example highlights the critical importance of moment selection for encompassing. The conditional moment in equation (4.17) is a univariate version of the SURE moments selection advocated in section 4.3.1. It unambiguously characterizes the relationship between y and x, which constitutes the defining characteristic of the alternative models under consideration and, therefore, plays a central role in the encompassing analysis. In sharp contrast, a marginal moment such as equation (4.20) is noninformative in this respect.

4.6 Literature Review

Except for textbook presentations, such as Davidson and MacKinnon (2004), much of the literature on MSM and its precursor GMM is fairly technical and exceeds the needs of the empirically oriented approach proposed in this book. Therefore, the list of references that follows is presented as reading suggestions for those who want to deepen their theoretical understanding of these two increasingly applied procedures, not as a prerequisite for our application of MSM to simulation-based encompassing.

4.6.1 Generalized Method of Moments (GMM)

The difference between GMM and MSM is that under GMM, the expectations of the moments under consideration are evaluated analytically and/or numerically (e.g., by quadratures), while under MSM, they are estimated by MC simulations.

Two pioneering GMM contributions are Hansen (1982) for a rigorous derivation of the asymptotic properties of GMM estimators under general conditions, and Hansen and Singleton (1982) for an application to nonlinear rational expectations models.

Additional theoretical contributions are found in White and Domowitz (1984), Newey and McFadden (1994), White (2000), and Gallant and Tauchen (1996). Some early applications are the term structure of interest rates by Dunn and Singleton (1986); representative agent models of consumption and leisure by Eichenbaum, Hansen and Singleton (1988); and temporal behavior of consumption and asset returns by Epstein and Zin (1991).

4.6.2 Method of Simulated Moments (MSM)

MSM relies upon MC simulations to compute the expectations of the moments under consideration. It was pioneered by McFadden (1989) and Pakes and Pollard (1989). See also McFadden and Ruud (1994) for bias corrections. A detailed technical presentation of both GMM and MSM can be found in Gouriéroux and Monfort (1996) as part of a broader presentation of simulation-based econometric methods. See also Gouriéroux and Monfort (1993), with a focus on panel data models. A few notable early applications are Lee and Ingram (1991) for time series models, Duffie and Singleton (1993) for Markov models of assets, and Keane (1994) for panel data.

4.6.3 Monte Carlo (MC) Simulations

MC simulations are widely used across econometrics. A basic textbook presentation of MC methods can be found in Davidson and MacKinnon (1993, chapter 21). Detailed presentations of MC simulation methods are found, for instance, in Hammersley and Handscomb (1964), Rubinstein (1981), Hendry (1984), van Dijk, Monfort and Brown (1995), Geweke (1996), and Richard (1996).

Obviously, random number generators play a critical role. For instance, see Devroye (1986) for an in-depth analysis of nonuniform random variable generation and Press, Teukolsky, Vetterling, and Flannery (2020, chapter 7), including access to the relevant software. For the timber auction application in chapter 6, we relied on the FORTRAN IMSL Stat/Library (https://www.imsl.com).

A critical consideration when dealing with simulation-based estimation methods is the smoothness of the objective function, as emphasized early by McFadden (1989) and Pakes and Pollard (1989). One important technique in this respect is CRNs; for example, see Liesenfeld and Richard (2008, section 13.3.5) for details and references on this topic.

5

Simulation Encompassing

5.1 Introduction

Let $M_1(\hat{\alpha})$ denote one's preferred model, explaining how a set of policy-relevant, endogenous variables are generated conditionally on a set of exogenous variables. As discussed in section 4.1, the main requirement is that $M_1(\alpha)$ be amenable to MC simulations. Presumably, $M_1(\hat{\alpha})$ has been produced by the application of its owner's modeling strategy, including such criteria as the economic and statistical significance of the key (policy relevant) coefficients in α and goodness of fit.

As discussed in chapter 1, such idiosyncratic criteria do not suffice per se to validate $M_1(\hat{\alpha})$ as a sound basis for policy analysis since they do not imply that $M_1(\hat{\alpha})$ can account for findings from alternative models $M_2(\hat{\delta})$, a necessary encompassing step to validate the use of $M_1(\hat{\alpha})$ for policy recommendations. Therefore, let $M_2(\hat{\delta})$ denote a model to be potentially encompassed by $M_1(\hat{\alpha})$. It could be a model produced by other researchers based upon alternative policy analyses and/or modeling strategies. Or it could be a simpler version of $M_1(\hat{\alpha})$, such as a nested one that assumes the absence of a specific conduct under scrutiny. This will be the case for the timber auction application discussed in chapter 6, when $M_1(\alpha)$ represents a collusive model and $M_2(\delta)$ a noncollusive nested version thereof.

All that is required to apply the simulation encompassing algorithm described in section 5.2 is that $M_2(\delta)$ can be reestimated under data simulated from $M_1(\hat{\alpha})$. This will be automatically the case if, as discussed previously, $M_2(\delta)$ happens to be a nested, restricted version of $M_1(\alpha)$. However, if $M_2(\delta)$ denotes an alternative model produced by other researchers, encompassing will require that $M_2(\delta)$ can be reestimated under data generated from $M_1(\hat{\alpha})$.

Application of encompassing does not require that $M_2(\delta)$ be estimated by MSM. Obviously, if $M_2(\delta)$ is nested within $M_1(\alpha)$, MSM estimation of $M_2(\delta)$ trivially follows from that of $M_1(\alpha)$, as will be the case for our timber auction application. It could get more complicated when $M_2(\delta)$ has been estimated by its owners, relying upon their own estimation procedure. Encompassing would then require either access to that software or MSM reprogramming. The latter might carry the risk of distorting some of the results to be encompassed, but this would by no means affect the relevance of the encompassing exercise. Actually, these two requirements apply to any statistical procedures, not just encompassing, dealing with nonnested models that rely upon distinct datasets.

Last but not least, we unconditionally recommend computing encompassing t-statistics for the individual $\hat{\delta}$ coefficients (instead of a global chi-square), as well as for any other univariate statistic that might be of interest, whether statistically (such as the M_2 goodness of fit) or for policy reasons.[1] The obvious reason for this individual approach is that it will greatly facilitate the eventual identification of specific encompassing failures and thereby provide essential guidance for further refinements of $M_1(\hat{\alpha})$. This key point will be illustrated in our timber auction application, where an initial collusive model M_1 failed to encompass a critical coefficient in the nested noncollusive M_2 but immediately suggested a key addition to M_1, producing a nesting model M_1^* that encompassed both M_1 and M_2.

5.2 Simulation Encompassing

As discussed in section 2.5, encompassing requires computing the sampling distribution of $\hat{\delta}$, instead of that of $\hat{\alpha}$, under $M_1(\hat{\alpha})$. Therefore, it essentially follows the same three steps as those used for $\hat{\alpha}$ in table 4.2, with two modifications:

1. We are now computing the sampling distribution of $\hat{\delta}$ conditionally on $M_1(\hat{\alpha}_{MSM})$, instead of that of $\hat{\alpha}_{MSM}$.
2. While MSM estimation of δ remains our preferred approach, we allow for alternative estimation procedures in this step.

Implementing these two modifications in Step 2 of table 4.2 produces table 5.1 for the simulation encompassing of $\hat{\delta}$.

Note: under MSM estimation of δ, step 2 is the same "inner loop" step as in table 4.2, but with $\{\tilde{\alpha}_{MSM,j}\}$ replaced by $\{\tilde{\delta}_{MSM,j}\}$.

5.3 HMR Simulation Encompassing

In chapters 1 and 2, we discussed our clear preference for encompassing relative to HMR encompassing in substantive empirical applications. That being said, the simulation approach presented in this chapter can also be applied to HMR encompassing. Actually, as discussed in our encompassing literature review in section 2.2.4, simulation encompassing has already been proposed for HMR within a likelihood framework, but it is far too complicated to be routinely applied outside the usual simple models used for illustration.

In sharp contrast, the HMR simulation encompassing procedure we propose here can be applied to any empirical model amenable to MC simulation under any consistent estimators. However, it is computationally significantly more intensive than the simulation encompassing algorithm in table 4.1 for the following reasons:

- Simulation encompassing relies upon the sampling distribution of $\hat{\delta}|M_1(\hat{\alpha})$ keeping $\hat{\alpha}$ *fixed*. Therefore, it requires computing $\delta_1(\hat{\alpha})$ only *once* for that fixed value.
- HMR simulates the sampling distribution of $\hat{\phi} = \hat{\delta} - \delta_1(\hat{\alpha})$, which obtains from the *joint* sampling distribution of $(\hat{\alpha}, \hat{\delta})$ given $M_1(\hat{\alpha})$. It follows that $\delta_1(\hat{\alpha})$ has to be recomputed for *each* draw of $\hat{\alpha}$.

Therefore, HMR requires two nested outer loops of simulation (as opposed to a single one under table 5.1):

- One to produce S_3 draws $(\tilde{\alpha}_k, \tilde{\delta}_k)$ from $M_1(\hat{\alpha})$.
- A nested one to produce S_2 new draws $(\tilde{\delta}_{k,j})$ conditional on to $\tilde{\alpha}_k$ to compute $\delta_1(\tilde{\alpha}_k)$. The kth HMR draw of $\hat{\phi}$ is then given by $\tilde{\phi}_k = \tilde{\delta}_k - \delta_1(\tilde{\alpha}_k)$.

The HMR steps are summarized in table 5.2, allowing for any consistent estimation technique for $\hat{\delta}$.

Table 5.1
Simulation encompassing of $\hat{\delta}$ by $M_1(\hat{\alpha}_{MSM})$

1. Outer loop: S_2 draws from $M_1(\hat{\alpha}_{MSM})$:

$$M_1(\hat{\alpha}_{MSM}) \to \{\tilde{y}_j\}_{j=1}^{S_2}.$$

2. For each $\tilde{y}_j$, replicate the estimation of δ:

$$\{\tilde{y}_j\}_{j=1}^{S_2} \to \boxed{\text{ESTIMATION } \delta} \to \{\tilde{\delta}_j\}_{j=1}^{S_2}.$$

3. Means, standard deviations, and t-statistics for individual $\hat{\delta}$ coefficients and other statistics of interest.

Table 5.2
HMR encompassing of $\hat{\delta}$ by $M_1(\hat{\alpha}_{MSM})$

1. HMR outer loop from $M_1(\hat{\alpha}_{MSM})$:

$$M_1(\hat{\alpha}_{MSM}) \to \{\tilde{y}_k\}_{k=1}^{S_3}.$$

2. For *each* $\tilde{y}_k$, repeat the MSM estimation of α following steps 1 to 4 in table 4.1 and of δ according to the selected estimation procedure:

$$\tilde{y}_k \to \begin{cases} \boxed{\text{MSM } \hat{\alpha}} \to \tilde{\alpha}_{MSM,k} \\ \qquad\qquad\qquad\qquad k:1 \to S_3. \\ \boxed{\text{ESTIMATION } \hat{\delta}} \to \tilde{\delta}_k \end{cases}$$

3. For *each* $\tilde{\alpha}_{MSM,k}$, repeat the simulation encompassing outer loop, following steps 1 and 2 in table 5.1:

$$M_1(\tilde{\alpha}_{MSM,k}) \to \{\tilde{y}_{k,j}\}_{j=1}^{S_2} - \boxed{\text{ESTIMATION } \hat{\delta}} \to \{\tilde{\delta}_{k,j}\}_{j=1}^{S_2}$$

$$\delta_1(\tilde{\alpha}_{MSM,k}) = \tfrac{1}{S_2} \textstyle\sum_{j=1}^{S_2} \tilde{\delta}_{k,j}$$

$$\tilde{\phi}_{MSM,k} = \tilde{\delta}_k - \delta_1(\tilde{\alpha}_{MSM,k}),\ k:1 \to S_3.$$

4. Means, standard deviations, and t-statistics for the individual $\hat{\phi}$ components.

5.4 Example 2.9.2 (Continued)

We applied simulation encompassing to example 2.9.2. For ease of reference, we reproduce here the MSM/OLS estimates of α and δ, as well as the binding function $\delta_1(\hat{\alpha}) = E(\hat{\delta}|M_1(\hat{\alpha}))$:

$$\widehat{\alpha} = \frac{\sum q_i x_i y_i}{\sum q_i^2 x_i^2}, \quad \widehat{\delta} = \frac{\sum x_i y_i}{\sum x_i^2}, \quad \delta_1(\hat{\alpha}) = \hat{\alpha}\frac{\sum q_i x_i^2}{\sum x_i^2}. \tag{5.1}$$

The simulated encompassing t-statistics are obtained by the application of table 5.1. We generate S_2 samples $\{\tilde{y}_j\}, j = 1, S_2$ from $M_1(\hat{\alpha})$ and compute the corresponding M_2-estimates $\{\tilde{\delta}_j\}, j = 1, S_2$. The corresponding simulated mean, standard deviation, and t-statistic obtain as

$$\tilde{\delta}_1(\hat{\alpha}) = \frac{1}{S_2}\sum_{j=1}^{S_2} \tilde{\delta}_j \tag{5.2}$$

Table 5.3
Simulated encompassing, Example 2.9.2

					Table 2.1		$S_2 = 250$		$S_2 = 1000$	
p_0	q_0	$\hat{\alpha}$	$\hat{\delta}$	$\delta_1(\hat{\alpha})$	$std(\hat{\delta}\|\hat{\alpha})$	$tst(\hat{\delta}\|\hat{\alpha})$	$\tilde{s}(\hat{\delta}\|\hat{\alpha})$	$\tilde{t}(\hat{\delta}\|\hat{\alpha})$	$\tilde{s}(\hat{\delta}\|\hat{\alpha})$	$\tilde{t}(\hat{\delta}\|\hat{\alpha})$
0.75	0.75	0.3045	0.1022	0.1014	0.0034	0.2471	0.0032	0.1248	0.0033	0.1951
0.75	0.80	0.2884	0.1022	0.1040	0.0033	−0.5393	0.0032	−0.6547	0.0032	−0.6697
0.75	0.85	0.2764	0.1022	0.1066	0.0032	−1.363	0.0030	−1.498	0.0031	−1.495
0.75	0.90	0.2489	0.1022	0.1092	0.0031	−2.240*	0.0031	−2.316*	0.0029	−2.460*
0.75	0.95	0.2192	0.1022	0.1114	0.0029	−3.163*	0.0027	−3.396*	0.0028	−3.269*
0.95	0.95	0.3016	0.1543	0.1532	0.0040	0.2816	0.0038	0.2356	0.0038	0.2805
0.95	0.90	0.3302	0.1543	0.1449	0.0041	2.293*	0.0040	2.283*	0.0038	2.394*
0.95	0.85	0.3504	0.1543	0.1382	0.0042	3.856*	0.0039	4.120*	0.0040	4.015*
0.95	0.80	0.3672	0.1543	0.1325	0.0042	5.188*	0.0040	5.378*	0.0041	5.297*
0.95	0.75	0.3824	0.1543	0.1273	0.0042	6.386*	0.0040	6.601*	0.0041	6.543*

$$\tilde{s}(\hat{\delta}|\hat{\alpha}) = \left\{ \frac{1}{S_2} \sum_{j=1}^{S_2} [\tilde{\delta}_j - \tilde{\delta}_1(\hat{\alpha})]^2 \right\}^{1/2} \tag{5.3}$$

$$\tilde{t}(\hat{\delta}|\hat{\alpha}) = \frac{\hat{\delta} - \tilde{\delta}_1(\hat{\alpha})}{\tilde{s}(\hat{\delta}|\hat{\alpha})}. \tag{5.4}$$

The simulated results for $S_2 = 250$ and $S_2 = 1{,}000$ are reported in columns 8 to 11 of table 5.3. For comparison, the analytical encompassing results from table 2.1 are reproduced in columns 6 and 7.

It turns out that this simple example is actually somewhat pathological, with very small differences between $\hat{\delta}$ and $\delta_1(\hat{\alpha})$ and equally small standard deviations (all of order 10^{-3}) compared to $\sigma = 0.1$. The net effect is that the simulated t-statistics are quite sensitive to even small simulation errors. Nevertheless, insofar as the only relevant question is where these t-statistics lie relative to the critical value of 2, we find that the exact and simulated t-statistics in columns 7, 9, and 11 lead to the same conclusions. The HMR simulated results present a similar pattern and are not reported.

We should mention that for the timber auction application discussed in chapter 6, the encompassing differences and standard deviations are much larger, such that the simulated encompassing t-statistics can be accurately estimated under $S_2 = 50$ (which is fortunate because that application is computationally intensive).

6

Application to Bidder Collusion in Timber Auctions

6.1 Introduction

Deviations from competitive processes often have major direct as well as indirect financial and legal implications. Detecting anticompetitive conduct and measuring the impact of such conduct are the subject of models that, as discussed in chapter 1, can at best be approximations of the underlying DGP since, among other problems, key components of agents' behavior are not observed.

In this chapter, we apply the MSM encompassing procedure presented in chapters 4 and 5 to investigate potential collusion at Idaho Department of Lands (IDL) ascending bid timber auctions from 2004 to 2015. We propose to address two key issues:

1. Was there bidder collusion?
2. If so, what would be an estimate of the resulting damage?

Our approach consists of two steps:

1. A tentative noncompetitive model $M_1(\alpha)$ will be estimated by MSM (actually, there will be two versions of M_1). As discussed in section 4.3.1, the most critical step is selecting the conditional sample moments $\hat{m}(Y)$ that are most likely to be affected by the suspected deviation;
2. The selected model will then be validated by the application of simulation encompassing, as presented in section 5.2, in order to test the capability of $M_1(\hat{\alpha})$ to account for the individual coefficient estimates of a competitive alternative $M_2(\hat{\delta})$, with emphasis on any such result that might be counterintuitive in view of the data evidence.

It is well recognized that ascending bid auctions, often referred to as "English auctions," are susceptible to collusion by bidders.[1] The intuition for the susceptibility is rooted in the fact that the collusive bidders, often referred to as a "ring," will remain active up to the maximal willingness to pay (WTP)[2] of its highest valuing member, just as that bidder would do acting noncollusively, while all other ring bidders do not meaningfully bid or refrain from bidding at all.[3] The collusive gain comes from the suppression of the bids by those who do not have the maximal WTP in the ring. The absence of an incentive to cheat on the collusive agreement comes from the fact that the ring member with the maximal WTP acts exactly the same as if they were bidding noncollusively.

As with any nonexperimental study, we do not have access to some information that the market participants possess. However, we have had several discussions with IDL staff, as well as an industry expert, to augment publicly available information regarding IDL auctions and Idaho timber.

Nevertheless, we demonstrate that, in spite of the data limitations, our procedure will produce statistical evidence of collusive behavior at IDL auctions, with an estimated loss of revenue (collusive gain) of $81 million over 12 years.

Chapter 6 is organized as follows. In section 6.2, we review IDL auctions and discuss the potential impact of collusion; section 6.3 discusses legal cases, relevant literature, and practical concerns. The data is presented in section 6.4. The empirical models for the IDL application are introduced in section 6.5. The results are reported in section 6.6. Finally, section 6.7 discusses extensions.

6.2 Idaho Department of Lands (IDL) Timber Sales

6.2.1 Description

The timber auction data that is the focus of our analysis pertains to sales by the IDL for the time period 2004 to 2015. As part of its statehood status, Idaho was granted 3.6 million acres of land by the U.S. Congress to fund public schools and other public enterprises. The revenues derived from the IDL's sale of timber are an important component of that funding.[4] Over the time span of our data, IDL sold between 210 and 250 million board feet (MBF) of timber per year.

IDL crafts a 10-year harvest plan. There is more certainty in the first 5 years about the volumes that will be offered at auction. Years 6 through 10 are more uncertain because of variations in natural factors such as fires and insects. With regard to defining the tracts, IDL looks for natural borders, prioritizing salvage areas, and transport issues/costs.

IDL sells stumpage at public ascending bid auctions to qualified bidders. To qualify, a bidder must post a performance bond equal to 10 percent of the reserve price, demonstrate adequate insurance coverages, and not be delinquent in any payments owed to IDL. By qualifying a bidder is stating a willingness to pay a price at least equal to the reserve price. Interested parties can attend the auction, but only qualified bidders can bid. The reserve price for the sale is stated in terms of the average price per MBF,[5] and bidding progresses in discrete increments in terms of the average price per MBF. The amount of the winning bid and the identity of the winning bidder are publicly known immediately at the conclusion of the auction.

Each timber tract offered for sale is informally announced well in advance of the sale. IDL describes all aspects of the tract, including exact location and geographic boundaries of the sale, species mix, volume of timber, estimated road costs, estimated logging costs, the amount of time that IDL allocates for the logging of the tract to be completed, and other tract features, including the reserve price. From the time of the informal announcement to the time of the formal sale announcement, potential bidders will cruise through the tract and offer comments to IDL regarding potential mischaracterizations by IDL. For example, a bidder may assert to IDL that its road cost estimate is far too low, given the terrain and other tract conditions. IDL personnel will assess the veracity of such commentary and potentially adjust the formal sale announcement. Road costs are particularly important since bidders receive one-for-one credits for road construction costs (based on IDL estimates) that can be applied against harvested timber.

Unlike the U.S. Forest Service (USFS), there are no small business set aside sales. As a consequence, except for some salvage sales, each IDL sale typically has a substantial volume of timber.

All IDL sales in our dataset are scale sales, which means that the winning bidder pays a species-specific price for the timber extracted from the tract on a per-MBF basis. The species-specific price is set by the winning bidder after the auction by allocating its winning average price per MBF across the species on the tract.

If a winning bidder does not log the tract within the prescribed term, then they forfeit their performance bond and deposit (where the latter is 15 percent of the sale price), and the tract is reauctioned. If there is a legitimate delay for the logging of a tract, IDL can extend the term by one year.

Timber tract harvest results are available to all bidders from IDL, although this may require a public record request. This mitigates adverse selection issues.

The USFS, Montana, and Washington State are all selling timber tracts in and around the sales conducted by IDL. In addition, there are ongoing timber sales from private lands. IDL ignores all other sources of timber in deciding how much timber to sell and what tracts to sell.

The species and timber tract products sold from IDL lands are, in order of volume, grand fir, Douglas fir, western red cedar, ponderosa pine, lodgepole pine, pulpwood, Englemann spruce, cedar products, western white pine, and small sawlog. The IDL timber sales are exclusively of softwoods.

Finally, IDL sales will sometimes have a special designation of "pole" or "pine" or "osr" or "pulp" in the sale name.[6] A designation of "pole" in the sale name means that the tract is not to be clear cut, but instead only the poles are to be harvested (as well as other trees needed to access the poles via roads for the harvest). "Osr" designates overstory removal, which means that only the tallest trees on a tract are to be harvested to alleviate competition for the smaller trees and thus give them a better chance for rapid development. "Pine" means that the predominant species is pine, and "pulp" means that the sale is predominantly wood that will be used for pulp.

There are only a few bidders who are viable bidders at pole sales. We have eliminated pole sales from the data.

6.2.2 Impact of Collusion

There is the obvious loss of revenue to sellers from effective collusion, as well as the diminished willingness of prospective sellers to offer their units for sale given the depressed prices. Furthermore, since IDL makes its auction results publicly available, private sellers of timber, assuming no collusion at the IDL sales, may reasonably rely on the auction prices as revealing important information about the value of their timber. However, effective collusion at the IDL sales means that the auction prices are artificially depressed and the IDL auction prices, therefore, do not provide reliable price discovery.

There is also the potential impact of collusion on auction reserve prices. In particular, note that the reserve prices for the IDL timber auctions are calculated using a residual value method that works backward from log prices, accounting for relevant costs in getting a standing tree converted to a log at a mill. However, log prices in the market have a natural downward bias embedded in them since auction winners do not sell their best logs. Moreover, if ring members are using reduced log prices to compensate one another for bid suppression, then reserve prices, whose calculations rely on log prices, will potentially be further depressed by bidder collusion.[7] Also, if auction volumes are diminishing through time relative to other transaction methods that use the auction prices as a benchmark, then the profits for colluding bidders, who are also purchasing through nonauction transactions, are substantially increasing through time.

It is important to also keep in mind that the participants in cartels, when conducting transactions with large customers, are explicitly discussing the bids that they are submitting to each customer. In other words, at the micro level, bid rigging is a feature of many effective cartels.[8]

In section 6.6.2, our MSM estimation of a collusive IDL model $M_1(\alpha)$ will also produce MC estimates of the direct collusive gains. Since, as just discussed, this only represents the tip of the iceberg, these estimates should be interpreted as conservative estimates of a potentially much larger amount of damage.

6.3 Legal Cases, Relevant Literature, and Practical Concerns

6.3.1 Legal Cases

There have been several cases involving allegations of bidder collusion at timber auctions (see the data appendix for references). Perhaps the most relevant for this analysis is *Reid Bros. Logging Co. (RBLC) v. Ketchikan Pulp Co. (KPC)* and *Alaska Lumber and Pulp Company (ALP)*.[9] The auctions of interest in this case were conducted by the USFS in southeastern Alaska, primarily in the Tongass National Forest. The period of interest was 1959 to 1975. The auction rules and format are not substantively different from what IDL uses today—registered bidders go to a central location to bid in an open outcry ascending bid auction. The court found that "from 1959 to 1975, ALP and KPC, the two giants of the southeast Alaska lumber industry, bid against each other only three times out of 143 sales by the USFS."

The Reid case motivates our empirical modeling strategy for capturing potential collusion at IDL timber auctions. Namely, only one of the colluding bidders registers for the auction. All other colluding bidders do not register for the auction. In contrast, Baldwin, Marshall, and Richard (1997, hereafter BMR) modeled collusion at timber auctions under the presumption that all colluding bidders registered for the auction. The Reid case implies that this assumption is not universally applicable in examining bidder collusion at timber auctions. Therefore, in this chapter, we presume that only one of the colluding bidders registers for the auction.[10]

6.3.2 Economic Literature

The economic literature is quite clear that ascending bid auctions are typically more susceptible to collusion than first price auctions.[11] Also, although the economic literature addresses the advantages of ascending bid auctions to first price auctions when bidder WTPs are affiliated, these results can be reasonably viewed as slight improvements around the second order statistic. In contrast, collusion can result in dramatic effects regarding the order statistic paid at an ascending bid auction. With regard to the estimation of collusive auction models, there are papers that have looked at offshore oil leases, milk procurements, timber auctions, and road construction.[12]

Some authors have assumed that first price auctions are wholly robust to collusion and then used that information to examine ascending bid auctions.[13] There is a good reason to believe that ascending bid auctions are less robust to collusion than first price auctions, but the presumption that first price auctions, with repeated auctions and repeat players, are wholly robust to collusion is a maintained hypothesis that is highly questionable. We discuss this fact in section 6.7.

Haile and Tamer (2003) have raised issues about discrete bid increments at ascending bid auctions. IDL sets the minimum acceptable bid raise to be $0.10 per MBF, which represents on the order of $0.40 for a mature Douglas fir selling for $1,000. Detail examination of 50 bid sheets provided by IDL indicates that, while increments are often larger at the beginning, they typically decline as the auction progresses. Overall, the bid increments and jump bids appear to be de minimis in terms of a material divergence from continuous bidding. As described in section 6.5.3, estimates of collusive gains (loss of revenue for IDL) obtain as differences between a reference revenue associated with a simulated second order statistic and actual revenue corresponding to an observed statistic whose unknown order depends on the simulated composition of the ring. The measurement errors induced by the bid increments are small and expected to be uncorrelated with the model regressors. Therefore, our estimates of collusive gains remain consistent but minimally less efficient.

In the economics literature, there is an analysis of the cost of entry for both mills and loggers. A logger is an independent contractor that converts standing trees to logs and then sells the logs to mills. Athey, Levin, and Siera (2011) find that entry costs for loggers can be consequential for their decision to participate in the auction, but entry costs are essentially inconsequential for the participation decisions of mills.[14] First, the IDL staff has informed us that it is rare for loggers to bid at IDL auctions. Second, the IDL staff has informed us that for an auction where the value of the standing timber is approximately $1 million, the cost to cruise the tract for a mill would be approximately $2,000, or 0.2 percent of the value of the tract. Our definition of a feasible bidder (see section 6.4) includes only those mills that (1) are of reasonable size, (2) are within 150 miles of the tract in question, and (3) have historically purchased timber species that are like the timber on the tract in question. In addition, given the unaggressive nature of IDL reserve prices, it is reasonable to assume that any feasible mill is going to incur the cost of a cruise. After gathering such information, the only incremental cost a mill confronts is to send a bidder to the auction. Overall, for a feasible bidder, the costs of entering the auction are inconsequential. Again, this is entirely consistent with the finding of Athey, Levin, and Seira (2011).

6.3.3 Practical Concerns for Modeling Collusion at IDL Auctions

Given that we are focusing on English auctions, where Vickrey logic applies, each bidder's WTP is assumed to be independent of the number of feasible bidders for the tract, L. If these were first price sealed bid auctions, that assumption would be unreasonable. However, IDL exclusively runs ascending bid auctions.

Mills are typically specialized. Therefore, even in the absence of collusion, it would be natural for some logs from each tract to be sold by the winners to other mills. Moreover, winning a tract provides additional benefits to the winners. Foremost, the winners can keep the logs that are best suited to their mill. They also have control over the timing of the harvest and can use less desirable logs as leverage in bilateral negotiations with other mills. All of this is fully anticipated by feasible bidders and accounted for in their WTPs. On the other hand, log transactions between mills provide an ideal mechanism for collusive side payments.

Freshly cut logs have quite a bit of moisture. Excessive drying before milling logs can produce splits and twists that greatly reduce the amount of recoverable lumber. Therefore, it is not sensible for a mill to have an inventory of logs that cannot be processed in a reasonable time period (depending on the storage conditions and time of year). The implication is that standing timber inventories are important components of any mill's planning.

Under the presumption of noncollusive conduct, mills need to be competitive. They know one another's specialties and production capabilities. They also know what their competitors have purchased from public sales (such as by IDL and USFS). Tract logging and transportation costs differ somewhat among mills. Mills have less information about the timber that their competitors might have obtained from private sales or other nonpublic sources. All mills need to have timber/log plans for the short and long term. Overall, consistent with the existing empirical literature on timber auctions, we will be using an independent private value model, allowing for inventory differences across bidders and auction-specific covariates.[15]

With regard to collusion at IDL auctions, it is unreasonable to think of a single ring of bidders across all auctions since mature trees are stationary objects and tracts are sold in different locations. Our stylized M_1 alternative assumes that feasible bidders enter a ring with individual probability p_i, independent of one another. There is no legal case history specific to Idaho that we are aware of that would lead us to model the probability of collusion differently. For this analysis, we are not attempting to identify the identities of ring participants. Rather, we are interested in assessing if collusion occurred at the IDL sales and, if it did, to measure the magnitude of lost revenue for the state of Idaho.

6.4 Data

The data used in our estimation consists of all IDL scale auctions from 2004 through 2015 for a total of 708 auctions. The summary statistics for these 708 auctions are presented in table 6.1.

Table 6.1
Descriptive statistics

	Mean	Std. Dev.	Min	Max
Winning bid	860,350	726,963	10,405	4,454,524
Reserve price	589,580	479,661	10,405	2,626,685
Total volume (MBF)	3,503	2,552	39	16,470
l_*	3.19	1.57	1.00	17.00
L	7.64	2.75	1.00	18.00
Logging cost	700,087	531,309	6,011	3,750,736
Term	33	11	3	60
Acres	279	191	4	2,212
Lumber price	181	23	134	232
Inventories	24,763	36,732	0	266,560
Winner business size	4.78	2.30	1.00	8.00

Variables definitions are as follows:

- Winning bid: The price paid at the auction.
- Reserve price: The publicly announced reserve price by IDL.
- Total volume: Measured in thousands of board feet (MBF).
- l_*: The number of bidders who register to bid at the auction. The data only contains identities for the top two bidders.
- L: The number of feasible bidders for an auction. A bidder is defined as "feasible" if (1) the tract is within 150 miles driving distance of their mill or their closest mill (for those who operate multiple mills); (2) business size is not the smallest (e.g., not 1 on the 1 to 8 scale); and (3) the top three species in terms of volume purchased historically by the bidder are at least 60 percent of the species, in terms of volume, sold at the tract in question. In addition, the top two bidders are feasible regardless of these criteria.[16]
- Logging cost: IDL estimate of the cost of logging the tract.
- Term: The maximum amount of months that the winning bidder can take to complete the specified cut of the tract.
- Acres: The size of the tract measured in acres.
- Business size of a bidder: Measured in terms of employment and coded from 1 to 8. A business size of 1 has 25 or fewer employees while a business size of 8 has over 1,000 employees. ("2" is 26–75; "3" is 76–150; "4" is 151–250; "5" is 251–500; "6" is 501–750; "7" is 751–1,000)
- Lumber price: The producer price index for softwood lumber (WPU081107) FRED St Louis.

- Bidder inventories: The amount of standing timber acquired from USFS, Washington State, Montana, and IDL in years prior to that of the IDL auction, within 100 miles straight line distance of the tract being sold and not to be harvested within the next 12 months.[17]

Our choice of 150 miles as the distance criterion for feasible bidders is based upon the following considerations. Feasibility critically depends on the aggressivity of reserves and on the strength of the lumber market. As mentioned in section 6.2.1, to compute reserve prices, IDL relies upon a residual value method, which starts with the price of the logs at the gate of the purchasing mill and works backward through the processing, transportation, and logging costs. Since log market prices change through time, the residual value per MBF changes accordingly. A yearly reserve index (defined as the average of reserve over total volume) reaches a maximum of 237 in 2006, bottoms out at around 98 in 2009 and 2010, and increases to 206 in 2015. It is important to note that IDL rarely has no-sales, indicating that reserve prices are typically nonaggressive, as further confirmed by the top two lines in table 6.1.

When the lumber market is strong, the effective radius for a mill to profitably bid on a tract will expand. Actually, the IDL staff has told us that the feasible hauling distance can occasionally exceed 200 miles. Accounting for the pro-cyclical variations of reserve and lumber prices, we selected 150 miles as a conservative distance criterion. In appendix 6B (concerning robustness checks), we shall also consider an even more conservative criterion of 125 miles.

Next, we turn our attention to the winning bid measured as a percentage above the reserve price, which we refer to as the "premium." We compute the following two regressions for the 626 auctions with at least two bidders (with t-statistics in parentheses):[18]

$$\ln(Premium) = \underset{(5.21)}{0.165} + \underset{(7.27)}{0.194} \ln(l_*), R^2 = 0.091 \tag{6.1}$$

$$\ln(Premium) = \underset{(8.03)}{0.424} - \underset{(-0.60)}{0.015} \ln(L), R^2 = 0.001. \tag{6.2}$$

It follows, from the estimate 0.194, that competitive bidding takes place among registered bidders (l_*). It is consistent with a story whereby an eventual ring would register a single bidder, an assumption that will be included in the baseline collusive model introduced in section 6.5.

A potential noncollusive rationalization of the large differences between L and l_* might be that feasible bidders who did not register were filled with inventories, while those who did register were short on inventories. However, an obvious alternative explanation is that several feasible bidders were part of a ring and were instructed not to register.

Table 6.2
Business size versus bidder's average inventory in MBF

	708 Auctions		
Business Size	Number of Auctions	Average Inventory of Winning Bidder	Average Inventory of Nonwinning Feasible Bidders
1	58	1,162	489
2	128	21,565	17,575
3	49	22,646	15,473
4	103	43,708	19,288
5	36	20,663	14,488
6	211	103,454	32,066
8	123	59,653	28,491

To provide additional insight into the potential impact of inventories, we contrast in table 6.2 average inventories for the winners with those of all other feasible bidders, as a function of business size.[19] A remarkable feature of table 6.2 is that the average inventories of these other feasible bidders is uniformly lower than those of the winners. This is exactly the opposite of what we would expect from the inventory-based, noncollusive conjecture presented here.

The facts that (1) according to table 6.2, winners typically have higher inventories (and, as we shall see higher mean WTPs); and (2) the fact that we observe 82 auctions with only a single registered bidder provides additional support to our working assumption that only the ring member with the highest WTP above R registers. Moreover, in the *Reid Bros.* legal case mentioned in section 6.3.1, the two defendants were the biggest mills, with certainly the biggest timber inventories. One of the reasons why the defendants were caught is that they acted jointly as a dominant firm, punishing any smaller firm that attempted to bid for timber. We are unaware of any evidence of such predatory behavior at IDL auctions. Nevertheless, it still is the case that mills with large inventories win more frequently than smaller mills. Thus, it appears more likely that the latter are invited to join the ring and, perhaps, are rewarded with logs at discounted prices. It follows that, in the absence of more direct evidence, equations (6.1) and (6.2) and table 6.2 support three of the key assumptions introduced in section 6.5:

1. The ring formation process
2. The inclusion of inventories in the WTP means
3. The inclusion of the normalized order statistics in the probability of joining the ring (namely, the higher is WTP the higher is the probability of joining the ring).

6.5 Models for the IDL Application

6.5.1 Baseline Models

IDL relies upon English auctions with reserve R. Therefore, Vickrey logic applies whereby registered bidders remain active at the auction up to their WTPs. In table 6.1, we found out that the number of registered bidders l_* is on average less than 50 percent of that of feasible bidders L. We shall consider two competing reasons for such a discrepancy:

- M_2 (noncollusive): Any bidder with a WTP below R abstains from registering. Registered bidders bid up to their respective WTPs. Obviously, to account for those cases when l_* is significantly less than L, M_2 would require that reserves be aggressive (which does not appear to be the case from the first two lines in table 6.1).
- M_1 (collusive): Among all the ring members with WTPs above R, only the one with the highest WTP registers. All other ring WTPs are effectively suppressed. This key assumption is justified by the following considerations.

First and foremost, as explained in section 6.1, as we lack fact-based evidence relative to ring operations, our objective is that of producing an inherently stylized version thereof, relying upon a careful data-based assessment of bidders' potential incentives to collude. This is a critical distinction from the collusive model proposed by BMR, whereby all feasible bidders with WTPs above R join a single auction specific ring with independent and identically distributed (i.i.d.) probability p and register for the auction.

Our assumption that only the ring member with the highest WTP above R registers for the auction is consistent with the *Reid Bros.* case and accounts for eventual large differences between l_* and L. Moreover, the regression in equation (6.1) is indicative of effective competition among the registered bidders, which would not be the case if l_* included several ring members.

Another distinction from BMR, as suggested by table 6.2, is that we shall allow asymmetries in the mean of the WTPs by including bidder-specific covariates, specifically inventories.

6.5.2 Empirical Models

Next, we present implementation details for two versions of our best-fitting collusive model M_1. As explained next, they differ only by the assumptions on the individual probabilities p_i of joining the ring. Thus, they imply a common, nested, noncollusive version M_2, obtained by setting $p_i = 0$. The available data is listed in table 6.1. The description that follows applies to an individual auction with bidders indexed by $i : 1 \to L$.

As commonly the case, the WTPs, denoted as V_i, the reserve R and the price P are normalized by volume and expressed in logarithms. The four covariates in rows 6 to 9 of table 6.1 are rescaled[20] to avoid imbalances and expressed in logarithms. Inventories are normalized in (0, 1) and ln(L) is divided by 3, so $\frac{1}{3}\ln(L)$ is also in (0, 1), as $\max(L) = 18$ (so either one can be used as eventual covariate in p_i).

We assume that the V_i's follow a normal distribution[21] with mean μ_i and variance σ^2. The WTP mean $\mu_i = \beta' x_i$, where x_i denotes auction-specific covariates together with bidder specific (normalized) inventories. The latter is included to account for bidder asymmetry as implied by table 6.2. As we shall see, its coefficient turns out to be highly significant and plays a critical role in the encompassing analysis. At earlier stages, we also tested for additional covariates such as regional dummies, but none turned out to be significant.

Obviously, the individual probabilities p_i of colluding are the most critical components of M_1. Actually, we considered two alternative nested specifications for p_i. In both cases, we introduce ln(L) as an auction-specific covariate in p_i on the ground that the greater the number of feasible bidders, the higher the incentive to collude since the gain from noncollusive play is a decreasing function of the number of feasible bidders.

Our initial M_1 version only includes that covariate in p_i, which is then given by

$$M_1 : p_i = \gamma_1 + \gamma_2 \frac{1}{3} \ln(L), \tag{6.3}$$

where $\frac{1}{3}\ln(L) \in (0, 1)$ since $L \leq 18$. However, as we shall see in section 6.6, it turns out that this version of M_1 fails to encompass three out of the six coefficients in the M_2 ($p_i = 0$) WTP mean with, in addition, a borderline t-statistic (-1.977) for the coefficient of the inventories covariate, which is a critical variable in view of table 6.2. Actually, it appears from columns 3 and 4 in that table that there might be bidder asymmetry in the probability of colluding. Specifically, the greater the differential between a bidder's WTP and the reserve the higher their incentive to collude since under such a circumstance, noncollusive play has the potential to seriously erode the high expected surplus from the auction that would be earned by collusion. This implies the introduction of a variable into the probability of collusion that measures the difference between a bidder's WTP and the reserve. Normalization of this variable is required for the probability of the collusion to live on zero to one. We presume each bidder has a reasonable idea of the distribution of WTP for a given auction. With this in mind, a normalization is simply obtained by dividing one's WTP minus the reserve by the maximum

WTP at the auction minus the reserve. We call this normalized premium of the bidder's value above the reserve, Z_i, which is between zero and one inclusive.

The probability of colluding is then given by[22]

$$M_1^* : p_i = \gamma_1 + \gamma_2 \cdot \frac{1}{3} \ln(L) + \gamma_3 Z_i. \tag{6.4}$$

Note that, by adding a bidder-specific covariate Z_i in the probability p_i, we introduce an additional difference with BMR, where p_i is only auction specific. To guarantee that $p_i \in (0, 1)$, the γ's coefficients are subject to the following constraints:

$$(\gamma_1, \gamma_1 + \gamma_2, \gamma_1 + \gamma_3, \gamma_1 + \gamma_2 + \gamma_3) \in [0, 1]^4. \tag{6.5}$$

In appendix 6B, we introduce an auxiliary one-to-one reparameterization that is free of constraints, enabling us to keep relying on an unconstrained simplex optimizer.

Before we proceed to the estimation and encompassing stages, it is important to emphasize that we have no first hand information on the inner working of an eventual ring (indeed no one has, except for the ring members themselves). Therefore, the p_i equation (6.4) represents at best an approximation of an eventual and inherently more complex collusive mechanism. Most important, it reflects what are bound to be the two major incentives to collude. As discussed in chapters 1 and 2, our objective is not that of testing whether M_1 or M_1^* are correctly specified. They are not. Instead, our objective is to find (1) whether the best-fitting model M_1^* can encompass its two nested alternatives, the collusive M_1 and noncollusive M_2; and (2) whether there might be finite sample mutual encompassing between M_1^* and M_1.

6.5.3 MC Simulation of the (l_*, P) Process under M_1 and M_1^*

Under BMR, the conditional distribution of P given L takes the form of a nonstochastic mixture of order statistics, for which there are operational likelihood functions. This is not the case here, as we are discussing stochastic mixtures under M_1^*. In sharp contrast, as we now discuss, MC simulation of both M_1 and M_1^* is conceptually straightforward, but it does require attention to detail. In this section, we present the three-step simulation algorithm for an individual auction:

- The first step consists of drawing the WTPs. Let the V_i denote the order statistics in decreasing order:

$$V_1 > V_2 > \cdots > V_L. \tag{6.6}$$

- The next step consists of computing the corresponding p_i and drawing ring memberships. The L feasible bidders are grouped into three categories:

l_1: those with $V > R$ and joining the ring

l_2: those with $V > R$ and not joining the ring

l_3: those with $V < R$

- The final step consists of transforming the pair (l_1, l_2) and the corresponding V_i into (l_*, P). It proves convenient to consider four mutually exclusive cases:

$$\text{Case } 1^{23}: (l_1 = 0, l_2 = 0) \Longrightarrow (l_*, P) = (0, R). \tag{6.7}$$

$$\text{Case 2}: (l_1 = 0, l_2 = 1) \text{ or } (l_1 > 0, l_2 = 0) \Longrightarrow (l_*, P) = (1, R). \tag{6.8}$$

$$\text{Case 3}: (l_1 = 0, l_2 > 1) \Longrightarrow (l_*, P) = (l_2, V_2). \tag{6.9}$$

$$\text{Case 4}: (l_1 > 0, l_2 > 0) \Longrightarrow (l_*, P) = (l_2 + 1, V_{r+1}), \tag{6.10}$$

where r: $1 \rightarrow l_1$ is given by (6.11)

$$r = 1, \text{ if } V_1 \notin C$$
$$r \in (1, l_1) \text{ if } (\cap_{i=1}^{r} V_i \in C) \cap (V_{r+1} \notin C).$$

Collusive gains obtain under case 2 when $l_1 > 0$ and case 4 when $r > 1$. Accounting for the lognormalization of WTPs and reserves, the corresponding collusive gains are given by

$$cg = Vol * (\exp V_2 - \exp R), \qquad \text{for case 2, } l_1 > 0 \tag{6.12}$$

$$cg = Vol * (\exp V_2 - \exp V_{r+1}), \qquad \text{for case 4, } r > 1. \tag{6.13}$$

These individual collusive gains will be computed at the MSM estimate $\widehat{\alpha}_{MSM}$ and added together to produce an estimate of the overall collusive gain under M_1 and M_1^*. Moreover, exactly as we do for $\widehat{\alpha}_{MSM}$, we can rely upon outer loop simulations to produce finite sample moments for such collusive gains.

6.6 Results

6.6.1 The MSM Sample Moments $\hat{m}(Y)$ and the Weight Matrix $\hat{W}$

As discussed in section 4.3.1, the selection of the sample moments $\hat{m}(Y)$ in equation (4.1) constitutes the most critical step for the estimation of the IDL baseline models since the MSM estimates will be the parameter values that best account for $\hat{m}(Y)$. Obviously, the two key observable variables most directly affected by eventual collusion are $\ln(P/vol)$ and $\ln(1+l_*)$.[24] Therefore, $\hat{m}(Y)$ will consist of the coefficients of a two-equation SURE for these two variables, conditionally on the eight auction-specific covariates listed in table 6.1, together with eventual regional dummies. We ended by settling on an unrestricted SURE, excluding regressors whose coefficients turned out to be insignificant in both equations. The end results are reported in table 6.3 for a total of 16 regression coefficients in $\hat{m}(Y)$. As the number of coefficients to be estimated is 10 for M_1^*, 9 for M_1, and 7 for M_2, we believe that these 16 sample moments provide an adequate degree of overidentification. As for the weight matrix $\hat{W}$ in equation (4.1), we use the 16×16 SURE covariance matrix of the regression coefficients.

6.6.2 MSM Estimation and Finite Sample Distributions

The MSM estimation of the parameters of the three models under consideration (collusive M_1 and M_1^*, noncollusive M_2) and the computation of their simulated finite sample means and standard deviations follow the steps listed in tables 4.1 and 4.2, respectively. We use inner loops of $S_1=500$ replications to compute $\bar{m}(\cdot)$ and outer loops of $S_2=150$ replications to compute finite sample moments. The MSM estimates obtain from an unconstrained simplex optimizer (DUMPOL in the IMSL-FORTRAN library) that has proved numerically extremely robust (foremost, with no failures to converge under numerous applications). The results are reported in table 6.4 for M_1 and M_1^* and table 6.5 for M_2:[25]

$$\max p_i=\gamma_1+\gamma_2\frac{\ln(18)}{3}+\gamma_3$$

$$\overline{\mu}/\overline{R}=\text{average }\mu/\text{average }R.$$

Table 6.3
SURE results

	Dependent Variable: $\ln(P/vol)$		Dependent Variable: $\ln(l_*+1)$	
Variable	Coefficient	*t*-statistics	Coefficient	*t*-statistics
Constant	1.3440	7.7430	1.4894	5.6767
ln(reserveprice/vol)	0.6471	28.2154	−0.1492	−4.3030
ln(acres)	−0.0518	−3.3918	−0.0117	−0.5055
ln(loggingcost)	−0.2423	−6.2770	−0.3188	−5.4638
ln(lumberprice)	0.7717	10.6468	0.6379	5.8222
ln(volume)	0.2859	7.0295	0.3723	6.0553
ln(term)	0.0902	2.8144	0.0073	0.1508
ln(*L*)/3	0.4511	7.5043	0.8237	9.0648
Sigma square	0.0478		0.1091	
R square	0.7757		0.1926	

Table 6.4
MSM estimation of M_1 and M_1^* $S_1 = 500$, $S_2 = 150$

		M_1^*: Collusive			M_1: Collusive		
			Finite Sample			Finite Sample	
		MSM	Mean	Std. Dev.	MSM	Mean	Std. Dev.
$\mu = \beta' x$							
Intercept	β_1	1.607	1.594	0.106	1.551	1.564	0.111
ln(res/vol)	β_2	0.629	0.631	0.020	0.651	0.649	0.019
ln(logcost)	β_3	−0.247	−0.243	0.036	−0.246	−0.246	0.033
ln(lumberprice)	β_4	1.009	1.013	0.065	0.965	0.969	0.059
ln(volume)	β_5	0.246	0.244	0.037	0.253	0.254	0.035
Inventories	β_6	2.023	2.009	0.189	1.723	1.693	0.157
	σ	0.087	0.082	0.026	0.064	0.063	0.031
$p = \gamma' x$							
Intercept	γ_1	0.144	0.160	0.061	0.344	0.347	0.056
ln(L)/3	γ_2	0.628	0.613	0.072	0.495	0.490	0.078
Z_i	γ_3	0.208	0.197	0.055			
Max p_i		0.957	0.947		0.821	0.819	
	f_*	27.27	4.401	2.222	30.74	4.984	2.364
Collusive gain	cg	81.27M	81.47M	5.09M	57.78M	57.35M	3.26M
% $V_1 < R$		0.488			0.478		
% ratio $\overline{\mu}/\overline{R}$		1.068			1.066		

As expected, the MSM values of f_* demonstrate the misspecification of both M_1 and M_1^*, with M_1^* marginally better.[26] We can think of many reasons why M_1 and M_1^* are misspecified: foremost, we lack fact-based evidence relative to the ring operation; we only know the identity of the two highest registered bidders; we lack information on private factors that might affect WTPs; and WTPs and/or the p_i might not be linear, among others. However, as discussed at length in chapters 1 and 2, the fact that a model is inherently misspecified does not imply that it cannot be used for policy recommendations (or else economists would be out of a job). This is why the encompassing test statistics produced in the next section will play a key role in the eventual validation of M_1 and/or M_1^*.

Next, we discuss the M_1 and M_1^* results:

1. Our most important results concern the probabilities p_i of joining a ring. All five γ coefficients are positive and highly significant. With $\frac{1}{3}\ln(L) \in$

Table 6.5
MSM estimates of M_2 ($S_1 = 500$, $S_2 = 100$)

			M_2-distrib.	
		MSM	Mean	Std. Dev.
$\mu = \beta' x$				
Intercept	β_1	2.191	2.165	0.135
ln(res/vol)	β_2	0.630	0.634	0.022
ln(logcost)	β_3	−0.227	−0.224	0.042
ln(lumberprice)	β_4	0.515	0.514	0.061
ln(volume)	β_5	0.356	0.352	0.044
Inventories	β_6	−5.414	−5.384	0.965
	σ	0.414	0.414	0.025
	f_*	256.34	7.271	3.735

(0, 0.903) for $L \leq 18$ and $Z_i \in (0, 1)$, we find that $p_i \in (0.344, 0.821)$ under M_1 and (0.144, 0.957) under M_1^*. For example, for $L = 7$ (mean value), $p_i =$ 0.763 under M_1 and ranges from 0.551 to 0.759 under M_1^*. These explain the very large and highly significant estimates of overall collusive gains (loss of revenue for IDL) under both models.

2. The key difference between M_1 and M_1^* lies in the inclusion of Z_i (individual normalized WTPs) in the probabilities p_i under M_1^*. Under M_1, all feasible bidders at a given auction share a common auction-specific probability of joining the ring. In sharp contrast under M_1^*, p_i are increasing functions of the bidders' individual WTPs. It follows that under M_1^*, the highest WTPs are also the most likely to be suppressed at the auction. This key factor explains the large and significant difference between the estimated collusive gains under M_1 and M_1^*.
3. Next in degree of importance, we find that the coefficient of inventories in μ is positive and highly significant under both M_1 and M_1^*, as expected from table 6.2. To put it in perspective we note that the mean and standard deviation of normalized inventories equal to 0.0929 and 0.1378, respectively. Therefore, average inventories increase the WTP means by 0.19 under M_1^* and 0.16 under M_1, which are more than twice the corresponding WTP standard deviation σ. It follows that mills with high inventories have significantly higher WTPs than their rivals and, as shown by table 6.2, are also more frequent auction winners. However, these high WTPs may not show up in prices paid due to bid suppression inherent to collusion. This will be

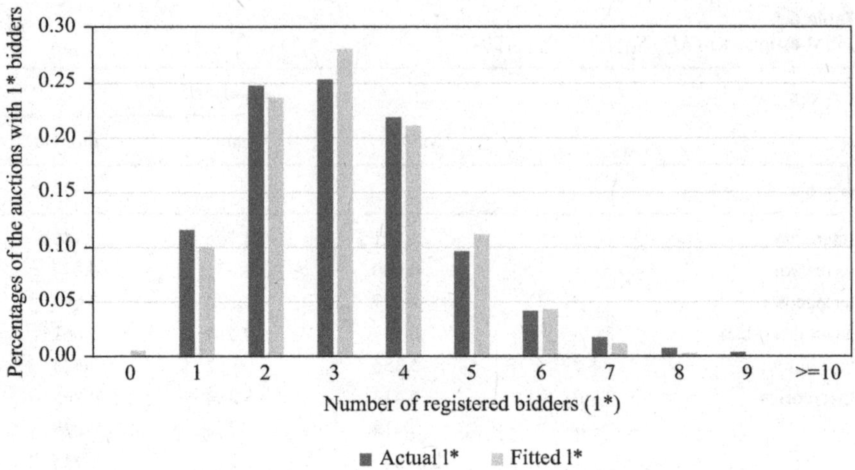

Figure 6.1
Histogram of the actual versus fitted l_*'s (under M_1^*).

especially true under M_1^*, where the probability of colluding increases substantially with one's WTP. As we shall further discuss in section 6.6.4, this story plays a key role in the encompassing of M_2 by M_1 and, foremost, M_1^*.

4. We note that the ratio between average WTP and average reserve is of the order of 1.07, fully confirming the notion that IDL reserves are definitely nonaggressive for reasons that were discussed in section 6.2.2.
5. Last but not least, figure 6.1 highlights the excellent fit between data and simulated l_*'s, even though the SURE R-square (table 6.3) for $\ln(1 + l_*)$ is only 0.19.

6.6.3 MSM Estimates of M_2

The MSM estimates of M_2 are reported in table 6.5 (column 3), together with their M_2-sample means and standard deviations.

We note that M_2 is nested within both M_1 and M_1^* since it obtains by setting the γ_i, and, therefore, p_i, equal to zero and reducing the number of parameters to 7. It immediately follows that MSM estimation of M_2 can rely on the MSM programs for M_1 and M_1^* by setting $p_i = 0$. Therefore, we can rely on the MC simulation of (l_*, P), as described in section 6.5.3. Since $p_i = 0$, however, it follows that MC simulations of M_2 always produce $l_1 = 0$ and cases 1 to 3, in equations (6.7) to (6.9), reduce to (l_*, P)=$(0, R)$ if $l_2 = 0$, $(1, R)$ if $l_2 = 1$, and (l_2, V_2) if $l_2 > 1$, respectively.

The two most critical findings in table 6.5 are

1. A large and highly significant negative coefficient (β_6) for inventories in the mean WTP. This is obviously a "wrong sign," in view of table 6.2.
2. A very poor fit with a value of f_* 9.4 (8.3) times larger than that obtained under $M_1^*(M_1)$, which has only 3 (2) additional parameters. It follows that under any model choice criterion that we can think of, M_1 and M_1^* would be chosen over M_2.

However, as discussed in chapter 2, the relevant issue is not one of model choice. Instead, it is that of verifying whether M_1 and/or M_1^* can account for M_2 and, more specifically, for the two key findings listed previously. In this respect, we note that while M_2 is nested within both M_1 and M_1^*, it is not the case that there is a function h such that $\hat{\delta}_{MSM} = h(\hat{\alpha}_{MSM}) + \hat{e}$. Therefore, as discussed in section 2.2.4, we are dealing with a situation where nesting does not imply encompassing.

6.6.4 Encompassing of M_2 by M_1 and M_1^*

As discussed in section 6.3.2, we lack first hand information about the inner operations of an eventual ring. Moreover, although inventories play a key role, we are likely missing other bidder-specific covariates that might also affect WTPs. It follows that we know beforehand that neither M_1 nor M_1^* could be correctly specified. Therefore, we see no reasons to test for HMR encompassing, notwithstanding the fact that running the HMR S_3 outer loop in table 5.2 would be prohibitively computer intensive on our SUNFIRE 2CPUs server (see note 25 in Chapter 6).

In table 6.6, we provide the encompassing t-statistics for the six β coefficients in the M_2 WTP mean, as well as for σ and f_*, under both M_1 and M_1^*.

We note that M_1^* encompasses all eight M_2 coefficients, including f_* and the critical negative "wrong sign" β_6 coefficient of inventories in the WTP mean. In contrast, M_1 fails to encompass M_2 on three of those eight coefficients with, in addition, a borderline t-statistic (-1.977) for the critical coefficient β_6. An explanation for that key finding runs as follows: Under both M_1 and M_1^*, we found that mills with high inventories draw significantly higher WTPs. However, we also found significant probabilities of colluding, especially under M_1^*, when mills with high inventories, and therefore high WTPs, are also far more likely to collude. It follows that there is a significant amount of "bid suppression" under both models (especially under M_1^*) to the effect that the prices simulated under collusion do not reflect these high WTPs. The only way that M_2 can account for these missing high inventories WTPs is by assigning a negative coefficient to inventories in the M_2 WTP means.

Table 6.6
Encompassing of M_2 by M_1 and M_1^* ($S_1 = 500$ $S_2 = 100$)

		M_2	M_1-distrib.			M_1^*-distrib.		
		MSM	Mean	Std. Dev.	t-stat	Mean	Std. Dev.	t-stat
$\mu = \beta' x$								
Intercept	β_1	2.191	2.658	0.176	−2.645*	2.554	0.225	−1.612
ln(res/vol)	β_2	0.630	0.554	0.027	2.884*	0.570	0.031	1.943
ln(logcost)	β_3	−0.227	−0.237	0.056	0.176	−0.207	0.059	0.336
ln(lumberprice)	β_4	0.515	0.741	0.081	−2.775*	0.703	0.102	−1.845
ln(volume)	β_5	0.356	0.399	0.070	−0.611	0.365	0.075	−0.122
Inventories	β_6	−5.414	−10.549	2.597	−1.977	−9.957	2.971	−1.529
	σ	0.414	0.249	0.097	1.709	0.268	0.107	1.369
	f_*	256.34	248.98	28.241	0.260	243.64	30.70	0.414

In section 2.5, we noted that t-statistics (in absolute value) under HMR are larger than their encompassing counterparts. Therefore, we can conjecture that at least two of the eventual HMR t-statistics for M_1^* would be larger than 2. In other words, as we knew beforehand, there is evidence that M_1^* is not correctly specified. Nevertheless, it fully accounts for the noncollusive M_2 results, to the effect that we can trust its key policy implication that some form of bid suppression is taking place and implies a very significant loss of revenue for IDL.

While it is clear that M_1^* outperforms M_1 in terms of encompassing the noncollusive alternative M_2, it is also useful to check whether it can also encompass M_1 (and reciprocally) for further validation. This is the object of the next section.

6.6.5 Encompassing of M_1 and M_1^*

For additional validation of M_1^*, we also checked whether it encompasses M_1. As shown in column 4 of table 6.7, it does. For completion, we also checked whether M_1 encompasses M_1^*. The results are found in column 8 of table 6.7. Except for the f_* t-statistic, which is marginally above 2, M_1 also encompasses M_1^*.

Therefore, there is virtual mutual encompassing between M_1^* and M_1, which might appear somewhat surprising in view of the fact that M_1^* encompasses M_2, while M_1 does not. However, under finite sample and incomplete information, such a combination of encompassing results can definitely occur. Nevertheless, in view of the highly significant γ_3 coefficient of Z_i under M_1^*, mutual encompassing between M_1 and M_1^* is not expected to hold asymptotically.

Table 6.7
Encompassing of M_1 by M_1^* and M_1^* by M_1 ($S_1 = 500$ $S_2 = 150$)

	M_1	M_1^*-distribution			M_1^*	M_1-distribution		
$\mu = \beta' x$	MSM	Mean	Std. Dev.	t-stat	MSM	Mean	Std. Dev.	t-stat
β_1	1.551	1.576	0.259	−0.095	1.607	1.773	0.234	−0.707
β_2	0.651	0.643	0.040	0.206	0.629	0.610	0.039	0.484
β_3	−0.246	−0.236	0.046	−0.228	−0.247	−0.275	0.044	−0.640
β_4	0.965	0.983	−0.083	−0.227	1.009	0.969	0.063	0.632
β_5	0.253	0.241	0.050	0.231	0.246	0.285	0.049	−0.791
β_6	1.723	1.607	0.631	0.183	2.023	1.749	0.271	1.013
$p = \gamma' x$								
γ_1	0.344	0.253	0.183	0.498	0.144	0.132	0.079	0.159
γ_2	0.495	0.608	0.250	−0.450	0.628	0.607	0.109	0.189
γ_3					0.208	0.236	0.105	−0.268
σ	0.064	0.066	0.050	−0.044	0.087	0.125	0.045	−0.835
f_*	30.74	17.41	14.94	0.892	27.27	9.18	8.41	2.151*
cg	57.78	55.26	4.85	0.518	81.27	80.12	11.56	0.099

We also note that in sharp contrast with M_1, M_2 is not a credible alternative to M_1^*. Its f_* measure of fit is 9.5 times larger than that of M_1^*. Foremost, there are obviously no way that data simulated from $M_2(\hat{\delta})$, with all three γ_i coefficients set equal to zero, could ever encompass the highly significant $\hat{\gamma}_i$'s for M_1^* (and M_1). Hence, there is no justification for testing whether $M_2(\hat{\delta})$ encompasses either M_1^* or M_1. It obviously cannot.

The outstanding encompassing performance of M_1^* leads to the conclusion that it captures the essential implications of an underlying unknown collusive process and is likely to represent our best approximation thereof.

6.6.6 Robustness Checks

In the course of our investigation, we ran a number of robustness checks, three of which are presented here by order of importance.

1. The assumption of normality of the ln (WTP)'s is commonly used in empirical auction models. Within our simulation framework, it is trivial to consider alternatives. Two such alternatives were implemented:

   (1) Student-t[27]; and (2) affiliation, whereby

$$V_i = \mu_i + \sigma(\sqrt{\rho} U_0 + \sqrt{1-\rho} U_i), \tag{6.14}$$

where μ_i denotes the mean of the WTP V_i, U_0 and $\{U_i\}$ are i.i.d. N(0, 1) and $\rho \in (0, 1)$. Results were virtually unchanged, as the Student-t variant produced a degree of freedom around 10 and the affiliation variant values of ρ are less than 0.075.

2. In view of the highly positive coefficient of inventories in the mean WTP, we expected that Z_i and inventories might be exchangeable in p_i. Indeed, we found that substituting normalized inventories for Z_i leaves estimation and encompassing essentially unchanged, although with an increase of about 10 percent for f_*. Therefore, we kept Z_i as a regressor in p_i.

3. As discussed in section 6.4, we selected 150 miles as a conservative distance criterion. Nevertheless, as an additional robustness check, we also estimated the model under an even more conservative 125 miles distance criterion. This reduces the average number of feasible bidders by about 14 percent (from 7.64 to 6.58) and its standard deviation by about 12 percent (from 2.75 to 2.41). The results can be found in appendix 6B (table 6.4B and table 6.6B). We find that the MSM estimates of M_1^* and M_2 remain close to their baseline values and the encompassing story is unchanged (actually the "wrong sign" M_2-coefficient of inventories is now -7.82 instead of -5.41 but remains fully encompassed). Obviously, the reduction in L implies a reduction in collusive gains of the order of 22 percent.

6.7 Discussion

6.7.1 Auction Design

It is difficult to imagine an auction design that is less resistant to collusion than the one used by IDL. This is a well-recognized fact (see Marshall and Marx, 2009). It is ascending bid, which is well known to be more vulnerable (as discussed in section 6.3.2). The identities of the bidders are well known at the time of the auction, and all bidding is publicly observable in real time. The reserve price is publicly announced well in advance of the auction. This auction design eases material monitoring burdens for a ring. There are auction designs for the sale of timber that have been demonstrated to be highly robust to collusion, such as the one used by the province of Quebec. Idaho should investigate alternative auction designs. Of course, the industry will strongly object, but that is, in part, rooted in the profitability of bidder collusion.

6.7.2 First Price Auctions and Bidder Collusion

It is not uncommon for researchers to assume that first price sealed bid auctions are void of collusion (e.g., see Athey, Levin, and Seira, 2011, p. 235, "we assume competitive behavior in the sealed bid auctions as outlined"), and thus that they can serve as a benchmark for evaluating the extent of collusion at ascending bid auctions. This is a remarkably strong assumption. From the public record, the vast majority of effective cartels have confronted first price sealed bid procurements by buyers and successfully rigged bids to elevate prices paid by buyers.

Second, we looked at the USFS timber sales in Idaho over the same period of time as investigated herein for the IDL auctions. We found 31 ascending bid auctions and 152 first price sealed bid auctions. The corresponding average (l_*, L) pairs are of the same relative magnitude as for the IDL sales that we studied: (2.7, 6.4) for USFS-AB and (2.3, 6.3) for USFS-FP compared to (3.2, 7.6) for IDL. If first price sealed bid auctions are void of collusion, then why are so many feasible bidders not registering for those sales? Our findings suggest that a leading potential explanation would be bidder collusion. Perhaps bidder collusion at a sealed bid auction, where the auctions repeat and the bidders are largely common across those auctions, is less effective than what we observe at the ascending bid auctions, but that is an empirical question for future research. Our point is that the assumption of noncollusive conduct at the first price sales appears to be a highly questionable maintained hypothesis.

Appendix 6A Reparameterization of the γ_i's in Equation (6.4)

The constraints to be imposed upon the γ_i's correspond to the four corner cases:

$\frac{1}{3}\ln L$	Z_i	p
0	0	γ_1
1	0	$\gamma_1+\gamma_2$
0	1	$\gamma_1+\gamma_3$
1	1	$\gamma_1+\gamma_2+\gamma_3$.

All four corner combinations need to be in (0, 1). This obtains by reparameterizing the γ_i's in terms of three unconstrained parameters (ϕ_1, ϕ_2, ϕ_3) in the following way (up to eventual rescaling):

$$\gamma_1 = [1+\exp(\phi_1)]^{-1}$$

$$\gamma_2 = \theta - \gamma_1, \text{ where } \theta = [1+\exp(\phi_2)]^{-1}$$

$$\gamma_3 = d_1 + [1+\exp(\phi_3)]^{-1} \cdot (d_2 - d_1), \text{ where}$$

$$d_1 = -\min(\gamma_1, \theta), d_2 = 1 - \max(\gamma_1, \theta).$$

As discussed in section 6.6.6, we ran a robustness check, reducing the distance criterion from 150 miles to 125 miles. The two tables below are the counterparts of table 6.4 and 6.6, respectively.

Appendix 6B Robustness Check: Feasible Distance = 125 Miles

Table 6.4B
MSM estimation of M_1^* $S_1 = 500$, $S_2 = 100$

		M_1^*: collusive		
			Finite Sample	
		MSM	Mean	Std. Dev.
$\mu = \beta' x$				
Intercept	β_1	1.694	1.749	0.072
ln(res/vol)	β_2	0.620	0.612	0.014
ln(logcost)	β_3	−0.257	−0.262	0.028
ln(lumberprice)	β_4	0.983	0.977	0.074
ln(volume)	β_5	0.264	0.272	0.029
Inventories	β_6	1.784	1.703	0.219
	σ	0.105	0.111	0.026
$p = \gamma' x$				
Intercept	γ_1	0.054	0.057	0.039
ln(L)/3	γ_2	0.705	0.689	0.060
Z_i	γ_3	0.232	0.240	0.051
Max p_i		0.965	0.961	
	f_*	29.03	5.589	3.346
Collusive gain	cg	63.78M	63.55M	5.09M
% $V_1 < R$		0.532		
% ratio $\widehat{\mu}/R$		1.069		

Table 6.6B
Encompassing of M_2 by M_1^* $S_1 = 500$ $S_2 = 100$

			M_2-distrib.		M_1^*-distrib.		
		MSM	Mean	Std. Dev.	Mean	Std. Dev.	*t*-stat
$\mu = \beta' x$							
Intercept	β_1	2.433	2.424	0.108	2.572	0.211	−0.658
ln(res/vol)	β_2	0.625	0.627	0.019	0.577	0.035	1.406
ln(logcost)	β_3	−0.211	−0.212	0.033	−0.221	0.055	0.170
ln(lumberprice)	β_4	0.561	0.568	0.063	0.654	0.100	−0.933
ln(volume)	β_5	0.371	0.371	0.035	0.362	0.064	0.138
Inventories	β_6	−7.815	−7.862	0.686	−7.003	1.531	−0.531
	σ	0.252	0.246	0.032	0.274	0.063	−0.356
	f_*	214.20	4.562	2.485	233.02	24.93	−0.755

7

Conclusions

Encompassing has been a major source of progress in other scientific disciplines, so it is reasonable to expect it to be part of economics. Actually, as reviewed in section 2.2, it was formally introduced in economics some 40 years ago. An initial objective was that of providing a unified framework for test statistics commonly used in economics, and it was clearly very successful on this theoretical front. However, it came at a significant operational cost. First and foremost, it was loglikelihood-based to provide unambiguous asymptotic definitions of the relevant theoretical concepts. Also, in line with classical testing approaches, HMR encompassing was based upon a null hypothesis of "correct specification," later generalized by DGM but nevertheless focusing on the underlying DGP.

However, a loglikelihood-based approach is often computationally intractable in serious empirical applications (except for linear dynamic models for which HMR parsimonious encompassing tests take the form of conventional F-test statistics). Foremost, tests centered on a null hypothesis of "correct specification" are too restrictive in contexts where the underlying DGP is unattainable, with the effect that any empirical model thereof is inherently misspecified to some extent. Also, as emphasized by DGM, a formal encompassing test requires not only a null hypothesis, but also alternative and maintained hypotheses, where the alternative generally represents the default option in the case of rejection of the null hypothesis. We don't think that this is a common empirical scenario when M_1 is clearly one's preferred model, obtained after an extensive empirical analysis and model specification search to the effect that its owner would rarely accept M_2 as a reasonable alternative (but one to be encompassed nevertheless). Actually, except for the specific "model choice" case, HMR do not advocate shifting to M_2, when M_1 fails to encompass M_2. Instead, they emphasize that an HMR rejection ought to be interpreted as an indication that M_1 needs to be improved further, if at all possible, in the direction of M_2, which is actually much closer to how encompassing is widely used in sciences and also motivates our interpretation of encompassing as "accounting for."

We believe that simulation encompassing makes encompassing straightforward to implement and should be part of empirical research going forward. It only requires that model M_1 be amenable to MC simulations. While it is applicable under any consistent estimation method, it is best used in combination with MSM, which is widely applicable. Foremost, the selection of sample moments required for MSM provides critical flexibility in the selection of those moments that are most likely to be affected by the issues under consideration. In particular, as highlighted by our IDL application, simulation encompassing is very easy to implement when M_2 is nested within M_1, as is the case when M_2 reflects the absence of the issue under consideration.

As a casual observation, the refereeing process for empirical economic work in recent years has become increasingly burdensome for all involved. When authors submit an empirical paper, it is reasonable for the editor and referees to make a number of inquiries. A central set of such inquiries is about the quality of the authors' M_1. Editors and referees will often ask for perturbations of M_1 to ascertain if there is a better alternative to the initial M_1 submitted by the authors, to ascertain the limitations of the initially submitted M_1, or even to understand the findings of the initial M_1.[1] It impresses us that much of this is a casual encompassing-type exercise. Namely, does the author's M_1 account for the findings of other conjectured models? And, as many authors of empirical papers in economics can attest, this up-and-back with referees and editors can take years as numerous "revise and resubmits" are requested. We argue that simulation encompassing formalizes this process and should be executed by authors in advance of submission. In other words, encompassing is an essential component of a "progressive" and/or "constructive" approach to the research process.

Our IDL application offers a great example of how encompassing can contribute to improving further one's preferred model. After extensive data analysis and careful selection of the SURE sample moments, we initially settled on an M_1 variant of the BMR model, whereby the probabilities of colluding depended only on the auction-specific covariate $\ln(L)$. However, as reported in column 4 of table 6.6, this $\hat{M}_1$ model failed to encompass three out of the six $\hat{M}_2$ WTP coefficients, being also borderline on the all-important inventories coefficient. Obviously, it was fitting much better than $\hat{M}_2$, but its failure to encompass $\hat{M}_2$ was concerning.

Whether from a referee or an attendant at a seminar presentation, a suggestion was offered: we might want to consider an asymmetric extension of M_1, whereby the probability p_i of joining the ring would also depend on one's own

WTP. Such a trivial extension would have been largely impossible to implement within a loglikelihood framework, as it would transform the nonstochastic mixture of order statistics used by BMR to a stochastic mixture. In sharp contrast, it was trivial to implement in our application since it required only the addition of a single parameter in p_i, leaving the sample moments and simulation of $\hat{M}_1$ essentially unchanged (a modification that took only a few hours of additional programming and cross-checking). This trivial adjustment produced our final model $\hat{M}_1^*$, which did encompass both $\hat{M}_1$ and $\hat{M}_2$. We argue that this is a spectacular illustration of why simulation encompassing ought to be a central and easily implementable component of empirical research in economics.

We also strongly recommend that simulation encompassing ought to play a central role in policy-oriented macroeconomic applications. It is generally understood, at least by practitioners, that the underlying DGP is out of reach in such applications and, foremost, that policy recommendations based upon a macroeconomic model are inherently constrained by data availability at the time that these recommendations are issued. In other words, they are based upon one's preferred model, as estimated at that time. This is precisely where the encompassing of alternative models would prove most critical. Consider, for example, the wide reliance on dynamic stochastic general equilibrium (DSGE) models for macroeconomic policy. In many ways, DSGE models lie at one corner of the inherent theory consistency/data consistency trade-off, with linear dynamic models at the other corner, as emphasized by such sources as Pagan (2003, figure 1) in a report for the Bank of England. While it is generally admitted that DSGE models play a central role in policy analysis, it is also the case that they are generally not robust against structural shocks (e.g., recessions), while linear dynamic models often can adjust more rapidly to such shocks. This is precisely why testing whether a DSGE model can forecast-encompass a nonstructural linear dynamic model could prove critical (and straightforward!) using, for example, simulations of the DSGE model under hypothetical exogenous shocks.

Relatedly, simulation encompassing could provide a great thesis opportunity for graduate students. Take any of the 100+ recently published MSM empirical policy-oriented papers and start by checking whether the corresponding M_1 can encompass a nested M_2 version thereof, absent the policy under consideration. Explore alternative moment selections to identify influential moments. Consider alternative versions of M_1 and/or counterfactuals. Whichever results emerge would indicate whether the policy implications of M_1 are robust. Foremost, all of this can be done under the sole condition that the models under consideration be amenable to MC simulation, and by application of the modular MSM simulation-encompassing algorithm described in table 5.2.

A significantly more demanding task would consist of testing whether one's preferred model M_1 can encompass an alternative model M_2 developed by another researcher. Two key issues would need to be addressed.

1. Foremost, the respective datasets would have to be reconciled. Specifically, any M_2 variables that would not be part of the original M_1 dataset would have to be imported and/or proxied since M_2 needs to be simulated under M_1.
2. The programs used by the owner of M_2 might no longer be available. In practice, one could substitute MSM for the original M_2 estimation procedure, which would include the selection of hopefully influential sample moments. Such an alternative would likely affect the M_2 results, but would also robustify them against unavoidable specification errors.

All in all, testing whether one's preferred model M_1 can encompass serious alternative models produced by other researchers might prove demanding but remains an essential component of a progressive research strategy.

We conclude our book hoping that it will provide economists with a fundamental and yet easily applicable framework to improve their preferred model through its capability to encompass (i.e., "account for") results derived under alternative models.

Data Appendix

1 Legal Cases

See *United States of America, Plaintiff-appellee, v. George E. Walker, Defendant-appellant*, 653 F.2d 1343 (9th Cir. 1981); *Reid Bros. Logging Co. v. Ketchikan Pulp Co.*, 699 F.2d 1292 (1983); *United States of America, Plaintiff appellee, v. Portac, Inc., Defendant appellant, United States of America, Plaintiff appellee, v. Howard L. Wolf, Defendant appellant*, 869 F.2d 1288 (9th Cir. 1989); *United States of America, Appellee, v. Champion International Corporation, Appellant, United States of America, Appellee, v. Young & Morgan, Inc., and Bugaboo Timber Company, et al., appellants, United States of America, Appellee, v. Freres Lumber Company, Inc., Freres Veneer Company Androbert T. Freres, Appellants*, 557 F.2d 1270 (9th Cir. 1977).

2 Data Processing

2.1 Number of Auctions

Our primary data was purchased from the Timber Data Company (TDC); our contact was Doug McDonald. The data purchased from TDC contained information on 3,157 auctions, including in eastern Washington, Idaho, and Montana by the U.S. Forest Service (USFS), as well as the states. Discussions with TDC resulted in a few updates to the data originally provided. In addition, a few corrections were made to the data based on direct information about specific auctions provided by Idaho Department of Lands (IDL) staff in response to a public information request from us. Details of these specific updates are available from the authors upon request.

Even though the focus of our study is IDL auctions, we used the data for USFS sales, as well as the Montana and eastern Washington State sales, to create two variables, the more important of which is the number of feasible bidders (the other is firm-specific inventories). Recall that one criterion for being a feasible bidder is that the top three species in terms of volume purchased historically by the bidder should be at least 60 percent of the species, in terms of volume, that are sold at the tract in question. Since a bidder can potentially be bidding at auctions in eastern Washington, Idaho, and Montana (state and USFS auctions), we used auction data from all these areas to determine what a bidder had purchased historically. For this reason, sales outside Idaho have potential implications for our analysis.

There are 2,961 auctions with complete location information and volume information. These auctions were used to calculate bidder's specialized species and bidder's inventories. There are 2,687 auctions with complete location information, volume information, and information about the size of the sale (in terms of acres). Within these auctions, there are 1,040 IDL auctions. The time period of this data is from January 2001 to December 2015.

We processed the data as described here:

1. We excluded data for 2001 to 2003 from the estimation in order to calculate a temporally consistent inventory variable for the years 2004 through 2015 (the data for 2001 to 2003 was used to calculate the 2004 inventory variable).
2. For the period 2004–2015, we eliminated auctions with incomplete location information, size information, or bidder information.
3. We also dropped one sale with an obviously miscoded size (e.g., the tract was recorded as 8,800+ acres).
4. We eliminated pole sales. To be precise, we dropped every sale whose sale name contained "pole."
5. We only kept the scale sales (there are 29 lump-sum sales and 55 ton sales).
6. There is one auction (104SID30990572), where Idaho Forest Group (IFG) bid against Bennett Forest Ind. Since IFG was a merger of Bennett Forest Ind and Riley Creek Lumber in 2008, we are not sure what happened in this auction, so we eliminated it.
7. There is one auction (082SID20253010) where the number of registered bidders was greater than one, but no second bidder's name was recorded, so we eliminated it.
8. There are auctions where the number of registered bidders was greater than one (072SID60980170, 053SID20290234, 081SID30370273, 042SID40990769), for which we do not have the second bidder's location information. These were eliminated.
9. There are auctions (092SID10150170, 043SID20290235) for which we do not have the first bidder's location information. These were eliminated.

10. We also eliminated one auction where the number of registered bidders equaled one but there were two bidder names recorded.
11. We eliminated one auction (052SID50980138) because we have no information about the first bidder, TAMARACK RESORT. This is a bidder different from TAMARACK MILLS, whose information we did collect.

In the end, we had 708 nonpole scale auctions.

An Additional Miscellaneous Issue

There are bidders whose recorded names are probably not firms, names. For example, there was one auction, 054SID40990383, won by "WILCOX, ZAIN." Initially, we were unable to match this name with a firm, but after some online searching, we were able to complete the information for it.

2.2 Variables Obtained from Data Directly

The definitions of the variables in this section were provided by TDC in the code book or based on direct communication with Mr. McDonald.

2.2.1 Winning Bid

The winning bid is the variable named *highbidvalue*.

2.2.2 Lstar

Lstar is the variable *bdt* in the TDC data.

2.2.3 Volume

Volume is the variable *voltot* in the TDC data. This is the total volume of timber sold at each auction (in MBF, or thousand board feet). This is the volume for all products.

There is another variable named *volsaw* in the TDC data. That is the total volume of sawtimber sold at each auction (in MBF).

2.2.4 Reserve Price

Reserve price is the variable *advalue* in the TDC data.

2.2.5 Acres

Acres is the variable *acres* in the TDC data, which records the acres to be harvested.

2.2.6 Logging Cost

Logging cost is the IDL estimate of the cost of logging the tract.

2.2.7 Term

This is the variable *trm* in the TDC data. "Term" refers to the maximum amount of months that the winning bidder can take to complete the specified cut of the tract.

2.2.8 Business Size

Business size appears in the TDC data as follows:

Business size 1 = 1–25 employees
business size 2 = 26–75
business size 3 = 76–150
business size 4 = 151–250
business size 5 = 251–500
business size 6 = 501–750
business size 7 = 751–1,000
business size 8 = over 1,000 employees.

There are 8 bidders whose business size information was missing. We tried to get the number of employees online for each of these bidders and define its business size following the same criteria as before.

- PETTIT LOGGING, J & M is a bidder that never bid as a top 2 bidder after the year 2001. The number of employees is not available online. So we temporarily set its business size as 1 and do not include this bidder as a potential bidder for any tract after 2001.
- MERRELL LOGGING, MARK employs a staff of approximately 3. We define the business size = 1.[1]
- HENDERSON LOGGING, STEVE employs a staff of approximately 2. We define the business size = 1.[2]
- HENDERSON LOGGING, PAT employs a staff of approximately 8. We define the business size = 1.[3]
- WILCOX, ZAIN owns a smaller logging company. We don't have the exact information about the company, but we define it as a business size 1 "firm."
- SILVICULTURAL ENTERPRISES employs a staff of approximately 4. We define the business size = 1.[4]
- FINKE LOGGING employs a staff of approximately 20 to 49. To be conservative, we define the business size = 1.[5]
- FULLER LOGGING, TIM employs a staff of approximately 2. We define the business size = 1.[6]

2.2.9 Species

The species sold in IDL, Montana, and eastern Washington, and by the USFS are not always coded in a uniform way. In the TDC code books (i.e., the code book TDC sent us with the data, along with the older code book for the 1983–1992 USFS data used in Baldwin, Marshall, and Richard (BMR)), we can find the names of most of the major species sold in the tracts. It has been confirmed by TDC that the old USFS codebook works for our data as well.

There are 10 species codings that are important for IDL sales—grand fir, Douglas fir, western red cedar, ponderosa pine, lodgepole pine, pulpwood, Englemann spruce, cedar products, western white pine, and small sawlog. They are part of our variable constructions for estimation. For IDL auctions, there are three species for which we do not have information: HL, RWD, and LPP. However, HL was sold only once in all the auctions of our dataset, and the volume is 190MBF. RWD was sold twice in all the auctions of our dataset, and the total volume is 60 + 165 = 225 MBF. LPP was sold once in all the auctions of our dataset, and the volume is 220 MBF. These species are de minimis in size. There are also some small-volume species that are rarely sold by the USFS, Washington State, and Montana, for which we have little information. Details are available from the authors upon request.

2.3 Variables from Public Available Sources: Lumber Price

Producer Price Index by Commodity for Lumber andWood Products: Softwood Lumber, made from Purchased Lumber (WPU081107) FRED St Louis.[7]

2.4 Variables Calculated

2.4.1 Tract Locations

The location information recorded in the original data from TDC is not in a latitude-longitude system, but rather in the Township and Range Survey System.[8] We transferred the data into a latitude-longitude system with this website (http://www.earthpoint.us /Default.aspx).

An example of the outcome of this transfer is given in figure A1.

In our data, we chose range, township, and meridian as input. We did not select "sections." We used the Centroid output from the website (see figure A1) as the latitude and longitude for the tract.

2.4.2 Bidder Information

The bidder information we sought includes bidder (mill) location, bidder's business size, bidder's established year, and bidder's closing year.

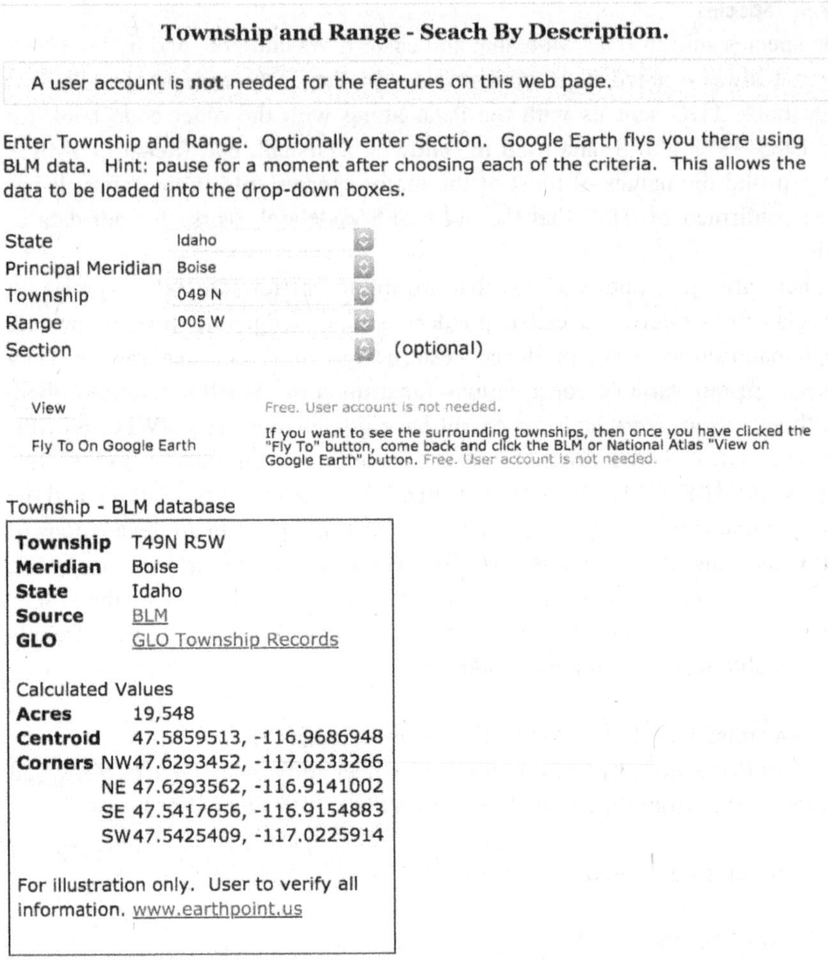

Figure A1
Township and range transferring to latitude and longitude.

Identity and business size There are 156 unique bidder names in IDL sales from 2001 to 2016 (January–June) that finished as a top 2 bidder. Identity information is provided only for the top 2 bidder.

We cannot find information regarding the following bidders online, and thus we do not know their location or years of operation:

1. BURNABY ENTERPRISES
2. M J M LOGGING

3. MATTHEWS LOGGING, LAYNE
4. WEBB & DORRY
5. DORY LOGGING, FRANK
6. RENEWABLE ENERGY OF IDAHO
7. TWO FOOT LOGGING
8. MR LOG
9. W E SULLIVAN LLC
10. DIRKS, BRENTON
11. BALIK, TOM.

All these bidders are recorded as business size 1 in the TDC data.

In addition, we do not have information for CROWN PACIFIC PARTNERS LP.[9]

There is one bidder named "TAMARACK RESORT." We do not have the related information, but note that there is one hotel with the same name.

Overall, we do not have information for these 13 bidders. Therefore, we have useful information for 156 – 13 = 143 unique bidders.

Miscellaneous Bidder Identity Issues

- There is another business size 1 firm named "M R LOGGING," which bid in year 2001 only once in our full dataset. This bidder may be the same bidder as MR LOG, but TDC recorded them as two different bidders.
- Two business size 1 bidders, MURRAY, L J and MURRAY, LEROY, may be the same bidder, but TDC recorded them as two different bidders. We are unable to find two different locations for these two, so in the mill locations, we kept only one location.
- Two business size 2 bidders, SUN MOUNTAIN LUMBER and SUN MOUNTAIN TIMBER, may be the same bidder, but TDC recorded them as two different bidders. We are unable to find two different locations for these firms. Therefore, in the mill locations, we kept only one location.
- Two business size 1 bidders, BROWN BROS CONSTRUCTION and BROWNS BROTHERS, may be the same bidder, but TDC recorded them as two different bidders. We are unable to find two different location information for them. Therefore, in the mill locations, we kept only one location.
- Two business size 1 bidders, LODGE LOG HOMES/ BALBACH and LODGE LOGS, may be the same bidder, but TDC recorded them as two

different bidders. We are unable to find two different locations for them. Therefore, in the mill locations, we kept only one location.

- Bennett Lumber bid under four different names. For 90 out of 99 IDL bids (or 112 out of 131 All bids), the business size of Bennett Lumber is recorded as 3. For the other 9 (or 19, including all bids, not just IDL bids), it is recorded as 5. In our data, we set its business size equal to 3.
- KINZUA CORP finished as a top 2 bidder in three auctions. It's recorded as a business size 6 bidder twice and a business size 5 bidder once. It bid under two different names. We set its business size = 6 in our dataset.
- Riley Creek Lumber finished as a top 2 bidder in 202 auctions. It is recorded as a business size 4 bidder 121 times and a business size 6 bidder 81 times. We set its business size = 4 in our dataset.
- TRI-PRO FOREST PRODUCTS finished as a top 2 bidder in 26 auctions. It's recorded as a business size 1 10 times, until the second quarter of 2012. After that, it's recorded as business size 3 bidder.[10] In our dataset, we set its business size = 3.
- TRICON TIMBER LLC finished as a top 2 bidder in 210 auctions. It's recorded as business size 5 180 times and business size 8 30 times. In our dataset, we set its business size equal to 5.

Locations We find 194 locations for the 143 bidders. We have collected all the possible locations that we could find online (up to May 22, 2019) and attempted to figure out whether the location was for a nonmill headquarters or not. For large firms, such as Boise Cascade, we can clearly mark some location as its nonmill headquarters. For small firms with only one or two locations, we do not know whether this location is just used for its headquarters (if any) or for mills. Then, we don't do any eliminations.

Overall, we mark five "pure" headquarters for Boise Cascade, Clearwater Paper, Idaho Forest Group, Louisiana-Pacific, and Potlatch respectively.[11]

Therefore, we have 194 − 5 = 189 locations as "mill locations."

Note: seven locations are listed on Idaho Forest Group's website.[12] We did not include the location "ST. REGIS, MT" since this was purchased in 2017. There are two ATHOL, ID locations, and we kept only one.

Firm longevity We find the established years and closing years in the following ways:

1. For large firms' mills, we relied on online information.
2. There are mergers or purchases during the period in our dataset. If we found the news reporting that merger or purchase happened in some exact year,

such as 2008, then we assumed that the bidder being purchased/merged was still bidding in 2008, and the bidder that proposed the merger or purchase or the merged entity started bidding from 2009. Of course, if we were able to find some announcement from the firms or news sources clearly stating the month and year when the mill would be closed or acquired, then we would strictly follow it.

3. If we were unable to get the established year or closing year online, we then inferred them based on our data. We assumed that the first time one bidder attended any auction in our data (All USFS, Idaho, Montana, or Washington auctions) was the time this bidder was established. That would be the "established year."

If a bidder bid before 2004 (and finished as the top 2 bidder) but never bid in 2004 or later (i.e., not finished as the top 2 bidder since we can only observe the top 2 bidder), then we assumed this bidder was closed before 2004 (i.e., we set the closing year equal to any number smaller than 2004).

A bidder may stop bidding in some year between 2004 and 2016. If we do not have exact information that the bidder was out of business, we assumed that this bidder was still open.

When we checked a bidder's open or closing information online, we mainly relied on Google Search and Google Map. If the searched result did not show that the mill was permanently closed and Google Map indicated what looked like a mill, we assumed that the mill was still open.

If we knew the exact open/closing month of a mill, then we used the exact month information. Otherwise, we set the open month as January and the closing month as December. For example, if we only knew that a mill was opened in 2004 and closed in 2006, then we set its open month as January and closing month as December.

Bidder species We set each bidder's specialized species as follows:

1. We found out all the auctions won by a bidder from *all* the auctions in our dataset, not just IDL auctions. The species and its code can be found in the "species code" file (available from the authors upon request).
2. We calculated the total volume of each species won by the bidder.
3. We ranked the species based on the total volume won by the bidder—the top 3 species that won the most (in terms of volume) are the bidder's specialized species.
4. If a bidder *never* won any auction previously, then we assumed this bidder was *not* specialized in any species.

We have no problem with identifying all the IDL species and matching the IDL species with the species in Montana, Washington State, and USFS.

2.4.3 Comment on Bidder Identities and Mill Locations

In the previous sections of this appendix, we described how all the bidder identities and their related mill locations were found. Given the definition of feasible bidders, the relevant bidders were bidders with business size larger than 1.

We had 42 unique bidders with business size larger than 1 (excluding the possible duplicated one, for example, SUN MOUNTAIN TIMBER). For these bidders, we have 82 mill locations.

2.4.4 Species Matching

If the top 3 species of a bidder are at least 60 percent of the species in terms of volume, sold at the tract in question, then we say that the bidder and the tract are "matched" in terms of the species.

2.4.5 Driving Distance

We calculated the mill-to-tract driving distance using an R program with a public package requesting driving distances from Google Map.

The program returns the driving distance between two locations given the fastest route. After manually checking some distances, we found that this was not always the shortest distance. Sometimes the shortest distance can be a a little smaller than the distance based on the fastest route (possibly several miles less).

We finally determined a 210×189 (tract $\times$ mill) driving distance matrix. Notice that we included all the 189 mill locations, not just the 82 mill locations for bidders with business size larger than 1.

2.4.6 L

L is the number of feasible bidders for an auction.

A bidder is feasible if

1. The tract is within 150 miles driving distance of their mill or the closest mill (for those who operate multiple mills).
2. Business size is not the smallest (e.g., not 1 on the 1 to 8 scale).
3. The top three species in terms of volume purchased historically by the bidder are at least 60 percent of the species, in terms of volume, sold at the tract in question.

There are other requirements for a bidder (mill) to be feasible:

1. the bidder (mill) must still be open.
2. if a bidder was one of the top two bidders, then this bidder was a feasible bidder, regardless of all these criteria.

There is one more restriction on L when we do the estimation: L must be no less than lstar. If the calculated L based on these criteria is smaller than lstar, then we set L = lstar.

Note: According to IDL staff in response to a public information request by us, Crane Construction and Deyo Bros are operators and could purchase sales of timber, but usually do not unless they are small, as in less than 1,000 MBF. Therefore, we do not include these two bidders as candidates for any sales with volume $\geq$ 1,000 MBF.

Notes

1 Introduction

1. This introductory chapter will contain very few citations to previous literature. Extensive literature reviews can be found in subsequent chapters.

2. Box, G. E. P., Luceño, A., and del Carmen Paniagua-Quiñones, M. (2009), *Statistical Control by Monitoring and Adjustment*, John Wiley & Sons, p. 61.

3. These will also be presented in chapter 4 for MSM and chapter 5 for simulation encompassing.

4. This is a critical difference with ML, which implicitly relies on an infinity of moments associated with the assumed distribution. This is the reason for the asymptotic efficiency of ML (under correct specification!) but also for its lack of robustness under unavoidable specification errors.

5. The requirement that $\hat{\delta}$, or any other M_2 statistic of interest, be computable under $M_1(\hat{\alpha})$ is inherent to any statistical test procedure, not just encompassing. When $M_2(\delta)$ consists of a model produced by another researcher, MSM estimation of δ can be replaced by the estimation method used by the owner of $M_2(\delta)$, so long as it is replicable. Moreover, eventual issues of data incompatibility between the respective datasets would need to be resolved first.

6. More will be discussed about nesting in subsequent chapters, including in section 2.4.4.

2 Encompassing

1. We also analyzed a more complicated scenario where the values of σ^2 from M_1 and M_2 are estimated. It only minimally affects the results reported in table 2.1.

4 Method of Simulated Moments (MSM)

1. All the summations in equations (4.17) to (4.25) run for $i : 1 \rightarrow N$, as was the case for example 2.9.2. This is not to be confused with the inner loop and outer loop summations.

5 Simulation Encompassing

1. As discussed in chapter 3, an exception to the univariate approach could be forecast encompassing for specific subsets of observations.

6 Application to Bidder Collusion in Timber Auctions

1. The empirical literature on bidder collusion has two main strands. First, there are studies of collusive bidding where the identity of the collusive bidders, and possibly the nature of the bidder collusion, is known from litigation. See, for example, Porter and Zona (1993) and Asker (2010). Second, there are studies without direct guidance from litigation that attempt to infer bidder collusion from the auction data, as is the case in this chapter. See, for example, Baldwin, Marshall, and Richard (1997), Bajari and Ye (2003), and Athey, Levin, and Seira (2011).

2. In view of the variety of idiosyncratic considerations that can affect a mill's private valuation, we suggest that it is more meaningful to refer to these as "willingness to pay (WTP)," but it is only a matter of interpretation and has no impact on the results. In all the formulas, it proves more convenient to use V to denote WTP.

3. See Krishna (2010, chapter 11).

4. IDL statement of objectives: "To professionally and prudently manage Idaho's endowment assets to maximize long-term financial returns to public schools and other trust beneficiaries and to provide professional assistance to the citizens of Idaho to use, protect and sustain their natural resources." (https://www.idl.idaho.gov/about-us, accessed March 16, 2024).

5. MBF stands for 1,000 board feet. A board foot measures 1 foot × 1 foot × 1 inch. Thus, 1 MBF represents approximately 2.36 cubic meters.

6. According to IDL, they include "Ton" in the name if it is sold on a weight-scale basis. Also "Salvage" in the name is used to indicate recovery of volume due to wildfire and insects. Although for part of this time period, "Salvage" could also mean an intermediate-sized sale no larger than 1,000 MBF and $150,000 in appraised value.

7. In addition, some components of the residual value method for calculating the reserve price are outdated and do not capture modern mill technologies.

8. See European Commission Decision of 5 December 2001 Case No Comp/E-1/36 604—Citric Acid para 123 ("Notes taken by ADM's representative at the meeting show that each undertaking was assigned a bidding price for orders in individual countries"). Also see European Commission Decision of 3 December 2003 case C.38.359—Electrical and mechanical carbon and graphite products at para 78 ("Regular contacts between representatives of the cartel members were necessary to ensure that the agreements made in the meetings were upheld in daily practice by all parties. Representatives also kept regular contact to coordinate specific bids made to large customers.")

9. 699 F.2d 1292, 1296 (9th Cir. 1983).

10. Also, to have all colluding bidders attend an auction would create unnecessary suspicion since the winning bid would appear low in light of the competition present.

11. See, for example, Marshall and Marx (2007, 2012).

12. See, for example, Hendricks and Porter (1988), Aradillas-Lopez, Haile, Hendricks, Porter, and Raisingh (2022), Porter and Zona (1999), Athey, Levin, and Siera (2011), Schurter (2020), and Bajari and Ye (2006).

13. See, for example, Athey, Levin, and Seira (2011).

14. See Athey, Levin, and Siera (2011, p. 245).

15. Following Athey, Levin, and Seira (2011), who examine timber auctions in regions that include Idaho, we assume independent private values. Athey, Levin, and Seira (2011) allow for two distributional types in their private value setting (loggers and mills), but since IDL staff has informed us that independent contractors (loggers) are almost never bidders at the IDL auctions, our assumption regarding the distributional source of values is the same as Athey, Levin, and Seira (2011). We also note that Haile, Hong, and Shum (2003) tested for common values at timber auctions and found that the evidence did not support common values at scale sales (the data that we used for our estimation is exclusively from scale sales).

16. There are other requirements when we calculate the number of feasible bidders.

   1. We assume the number of feasible bidders is larger than or equal to l_*. When L is smaller than l_*, which suggests that our criteria used for the definition of feasible bidders (and our subsequent estimate of collusive gain) might be conservative, we set $L = l_*$. We have 40 out of 708 auctions where L is smaller than l_*.
   2. Pole bidders (McFarland, Bell, J. H. Baxter, Stella-Jones, and Carney) will never be feasible bidders for a nonpole sale.

17. Data from 2001 to 2003 was used to compute 2004 inventories.

18. The joint regression is given by

$$\ln(Premium) = \underset{(5.11)}{0.282} + \underset{(7.98)}{0.214}\ln(l_*) - \underset{(-2.81)}{0.070}\ \ln(L), R^2 = 0.103.$$

19. There are no mills of business size 7.

20. The respective scale factions are 10^2 for acres and lumber price, 10^4 for volume, and 10^6 for logging cost. Under logarithms, such rescaling does not affect the covariate coefficients, only the intercepts.

21. As discussed in section 6.6.6, two alternative assumptions (Student-*t*, affiliation) were also implemented, but they produced virtually unchanged results.

22. As we shall see, these normalizations offer two key advantages: (1) at the cost of a simple reparameterization for p_i, it allows for unconstrained optimization; and (2) as opposed to the logistic specification used in BMR, our parameterization offers the advantage that $p_i = 0$ is trivially nested within M_1.

23. An alternative case 1 option is $(1, R)$; that is, conditional on $V_1 > R$. As the simulation frequency of case 1 is less than 0.5 percent, our MSM results remain virtually unchanged. Moreover, case 1 implies no collusive gain anyway.

24. We use $\ln(1 + l_*)$ instead of $\ln(l_*)$ to cover the very unlikely cases (typically less than 0.5 percent) where a simulated l_* would be zero under case 1.

25. All the computations reported in this chapter were run on a SUNFIRE X42000 M2 server with 4 GB RAM, 2 CPUs, Dual-Core AMD Opteron Processor 2220 and 16 GB of space. MSM estimation takes about 3 minutes of CPU time. The computation of the MSM sampling distributions and encompassing statistics ($S_1 = 500$ and $S_2 = 150$) takes about 8 hours of CPU time each. HMR encompassing would multiply these 8 hours by the factor S_3. Obviously, parallel or distributed computing would dramatically reduce computing time.

26. Under correct specification, f_* would be asymptotically distributed as a $\chi^2(r)$, where r denotes the "degree of overidentification," 6 for M_1^* and 7 for M_1, respectively. The corresponding asymptotic means and standard deviations would be (6, 3.46) for M_1^* and (7, 3.74) for M_1. The asymptotic critical values would be 12.59 for M_1^* and 14.07 for M_1 against simulated finite values of 8.62 and 9.20, respectively. As we discuss complex stochastic mixture models, our finite sample values could still be quite distant from their asymptotic counterparts.

27. The fact that the expectation of the exponential of a Student-*t* is infinite is irrelevant from a simulation perspective and serves only as an approximation of fat tails.

7 Conclusions

1. Editors or referees sometimes request that authors demonstrate that their model, M_1, is the DGP. It would be our recommendation to just submit the article to a different journal in this case since that request makes absolutely no sense.

Data Appendix

1. https://www.manta.com/c/mmdsgl8/merrell-logging-inc.
2. https://www.manta.com/c/mm7pt81/steve-henderson-logging-inc.
3. https://www.manta.com/c/mmfbq0p/pat-henderson.
4. https://www.manta.com/c/mmf15h9/silvicultural-enterprises-inc.
5. https://www.manta.com/c/mmg8tmw/finke-logging-co-inc.
6. https://www.manta.com/c/mm5g9sv/tim-fuller-logging-llc.
7. https://fred.stlouisfed.org/series/WPU0811.
8. http://www.jsu.edu/dept/geography/mhill/phygeogone/trprac.html.
9. "It filed for chapter 11 bankruptcy in June 2003, with its remaining assets, 520,000 acres (2,100 km^2) in Washington and Oregon, taken over by creditors in December 2004, who formed Cascade Timberlands, LLC" (https://en.wikipedia.org/wiki/Crown_Pacific_Partners).
10. Whether business size = 1 or something else is an important criterion for selecting feasible bidders. So long as we can observe a seemingly sensible direction to determine the bidder's business size, we will follow that. For example, if the business size of a bidder changed to be a number larger than 1 after the year 2009 and never changed to be 1 again, then we just assume that the business size changed. If its business size changed to be 1 again, then we take the observed business size larger than 1 as a mistake in the data.
11. Marking a location as a nonmill headquarters affects the feasible bidders in many auctions since they are close to many tracts.
12. https://idfg.com/mill-directions/.

References

Aradillas-Lopez, A., Haile, P., Hendricks K., Porter, R., and Raisingh, D. "Testing Competition in Common Value Auctions: The Case of U.S. Offshore Oil and Gas Lease Auctions," Univ. of Wisconsin Dept of Econ Working Paper, July, 2022, accessed Nov 7, 2024. https://users.ssc.wisc.edu/hendrick/working%20papers/ALHHPR_TestingCompetitionCVOffshoreAuctions_Draft_Jul2022.pdf

Asker, J. (2010). "A Study of the Internal Organization of a Bidding Cartel." *American Economic Review* 100(3), 724–762.

Athey, S., Levin, J., and Seira, E. (2011). "Comparing Open and Sealed Bid Auctions: Evidence from Timber Auctions." *Quarterly Journal of Economics* 126(1), 207–257.

Bajari, P., and Ye, L. (2003). "Deciding between Competition and Collusion." *Review of Economics and Statistics* 85(4), 971–989.

Baldwin, L. H., Marshall, R. C., and Richard, J. F. (1997). "Bidder Collusion at Forest Service Timber Sales." *Journal of Political Economy* 105(4), 657–699.

Bates, J. M., and Granger, C. W. J. (1969). "The Combination of Forecasts." *Operations Research Quarterly* 20(4), 451–468.

Blackwell, D. (1951). "Comparison of Experiments," in *Proceedings of the Second Berkeley Symposium on Mathematical Statistics and Probability*, 93–102. Berkeley: University of California Press.

Blackwell, D. (1953). "Equivalent Comparisons of Experiments." *Annals of Mathematical Statistics* 24(2), 265–272.

Campos, J., Ericsson, N. R., and Hendry, D. F. (2005). "Introduction." In J. Campos, N. R. Ericsson, and D. F. Hendry (eds.), *General-to-Specific Modeling*, Volume I, xi–xci. Cheltenham, UK: Edward Elgar.

Chong, Y. Y., and Hendry, D. F. (1986). "Econometric Evaluation of Linear Macro-Economic Models." *Review of Economic Studies* 53(4), 671–690.

Clements, M. P., and Hendry, D. F. (1993). "On the Limitations of Comparing Mean Square Forecast Errors." *Journal of Forecasting* 12(8), 617–637.

Cox, D. R. (1961). "Tests of Separate Families of Hypotheses," in *Proceedings of the Fourth Berkeley Symposium on Mathematical Statistics and Probability*, Vol. 1, 105–123. Berkeley: University of California Press.

Cox, D. R. (1962). "Further Results on Tests of Separate Families of Hypotheses." *Journal of the Royal Statistical Society. Series B* 24(2), 406–424.

Davidson, R., and MacKinnon, J. G. (1981). "Several Tests for Model Specification in the Presence of Alternative Hypotheses." *Econometrica* 49(3), 781–793.

Davidson, R., and MacKinnon, J. G. (1993). *Estimation and Inference in Econometrics*. Oxford: Oxford University Press.

Davidson, R., and MacKinnon, J. G. (2004). *Econometric Theory and Methods*. Oxford: Oxford University Press.

Davidson, J. E. H., Hendry, D. F., Srba, F., and Yeo, S. (1978). "Econometric Modelling of the Aggregate Time-Series Relationship between Consumers' Expenditure and Income in the United Kingdom." *Economic Journal* 88(352), 661–692.

Devroye, L. (1986). *Non-Uniform Random Variable Generation*. New York: Springer-Verlag.

Diebold, F. X. (1989). "Forecast Combination and Encompassing: Reconciling Two Divergent Literatures." *International Journal of Forecasting* 5(4), 589–592.

Diebold, F. X., and Mariano, R. S. (1995). "Comparing Predictive Accuracy." *Journal of Business & Economic Statistics* 13(3), 253–263.

Dhaene, G. (1997). "Encompassing Formulation, Properties and Testing." *Lecture Notes in Economics and Mathematical Systems* (446), Berlin: Springer.

Dhaene, G., Gouriéroux, C., and Scaillet, O. (1998). "Instrumental Models and Indirect Encompassing." *Econometrica* 66(3), 673–688.

Domowitz, I., and White, H. (1982). "Misspecified Models with Dependent Observations." *Journal of Econometrics* 20(1), 35–58.

Doornik, J. A. (2009). "Autometrics." In J. L. Castle and N. Shephard (eds.), *The Methodology and Practice of Econometrics*, 88–121. Oxford: Oxford University Press.

Duffie, D., and Singleton, K. J. (1993). "Simulated Moments Estimation of Markov Models of Asset Prices." *Econometrica* 61(4), 929–952.

Dunn, K. B., and K. J. Singleton (1986). "Modeling the Term Structure of Interest Rates under Non-separable Utility and Durability of Goods." *Journal of Financial Economics* 17(1), 27–55.

Dunnett, C. W., and Sobel, M. (1954). "A Bivariate Generalization of Student's t-Distribution, with Tables for Certain Special Cases." *Biometrika* 41(1/2), 153–169.

Eichenbaum, M. S., Hansen, L. P., and Singleton, K. J. (1988). "A Time Series Analysis of Representative Agent Models of Consumption and Leisure Choice under Uncertainty." *Quarterly Journal of Economics* 103(1), 51–78.

Engle R. F., Hendry, D. F., and Richard, J. F. (1983). "Exogencity." *Econometrica* 51(2), 277–304.

Epstein, L.G., and Zin, S. E. (1991). "Substitution, Risk Aversion, and the Temporal Behavior of Consumption and Asset Returns: an Empirical Analysis." *Journal of Political Economy* 99(2), 263–286.

Ericsson, N. R. (1992). "Parameter Constancy, Mean Square Forecast Errors, and Measuring Forecast Performance: An Exposition, Extensions, and Illustration." *Journal of Policy Modeling* 14(4), 465–495.

Ericsson, N. R. (1993). "On the Limitations of Comparing Mean Square Forecast Errors: Clarifications and Extensions." *Journal of Forecasting* 12(8), 644–651.

Ericsson, N. R., and Marquez, J. (1993). "Encompassing the Forecasts of U.S. Trade Balance Models." *Review of Economics and Statistics* 75(1), 19–31.

Fair, R. C., and Shiller, R. J. (1989). "The Informational Content of Ex Ante Forecasts." *Review of Economics and Statistics* 71(2), 325–331.

Ermini, L., and Hendry, D. F. (2008). "Log Income vs. Linear Income: An Application of the Encompassing Principle." *Oxford Bulletin of Economics and Statistics* 70 (s1), 807–827.

Florens, J. P. (1990). "Parameter Sufficiency and Model Encompassing." In *Essays in Honor of Edmond Malinvaud*, Paul Champsaur (ed.), Vol. 3, 115–136. Cambridge, MA: MIT Press.

Florens, J. P., and Mouchart, M. (1989). "Bayesian Specification Tests." In B. Cornet and H. Tulkens (eds.), *Contributions to Operations Research and Economics*, 467–490, Cambridge, MA: MIT Press.

Florens, J. P., and Mouchart, M. (1993). "Bayesian Testing and Testing Bayesians." In G. S. Maddala, C. R. Rao, and H. D. Vinod (eds.), *the Handbook of Statistics*, Vol. 11, 303–334. North Holland, Amsterdam: Elsevier Science Publishers B. V.

Florens, J. P., Hendry, D. F., and Richard, J. F. (1996). "Encompassing and Specificity." *Econometric Theory* 12(4), 620–656.

Frank, A., and Gleiser, M. (2023). "The Story of Our Universe May Be Starting to Unravel." *The New York Times*, September 2, https://www.nytimes.com/2023/09/02/opinion/cosmology-crisis-webb-telescope.html

Gallant, A. R., and Tauchen, G. (1996). "Which Moments to Match?." *Econometric Theory* 12(4), 657–681.

Geweke, J. (1996). "Monte Carlo Simulation and Numerical Integration." In H. M. Anman, D. A. Kendrick, and J. Rust (eds.), *Handbook of Computational Economics*, Vol 1, 731–800. New York: North-Holland.

Giacomini, R., and White, H. (2006). "Tests of Conditional Predictive Ability." *Econometrica* 74(6), 1545–1578.

Godfrey, L. G. (1983). "Testing Non-Nested Models after Estimation by Instrumental Variables or Least Squares." *Econometrica* 51(2), 355–365.

Gouriéroux, C., and Monfort, A. (1993). "Simulation Based Inference: A Survey with Special Reference to Panel Data Models." *Journal of Econometrics* 59(1–2), 5–33.

Gouriéroux, C., and Monfort, A. (1995). "Testing, Encompassing, and Simulating Dynamic Econometric Models." *Econometric Theory* 11(2), 195–228.

Gouriéroux, C., and Monfort, A. (1996). Simulation-Based Econometric Methods, *CORE lectures*. Oxford: Oxford University Press.

Gouriéroux, C., Monfort, A., and Renault, E. (1993). "Indirect Inference." *Journal of Applied Econometrics* 8, S85–S118.

Gouriéroux, C., Monfort, A., and Trognon, A. (1983). "Testing Nested or Non-nested Hypotheses." *Journal of Econometrics* 21(1), 83–115.

Govaerts, B., Hendry, D. F., and Richard, J. F. (1994). "Encompassing in Stationary Linear Dynamic Models." *Journal of Econometrics* 63(1), 245–270.

Haile, P. A., Hong, H. and Shum, M. (2003). "Nonparametric Tests for Common Values at First-Price Sealed-Bid Auctions." NBER Working Paper No. w10105. https://ssrn.com/abstract=https://ssrn.com/abstract=468792468792.

Haile, P. A., and Tamer, E. (2003). "Inference with an Incomplete Model of English Auctions." *Journal of Political Economy* 111(1), 1–51.

Hammersley, J. M., and Handscomb, D. C. (1964). *Monte Carlo Methods*. London: Methuen.

Hansen, L. P. (1982). "Large Sample Properties of Generalized Method of Moments Estimators." *Econometrica* 50(4), 1029–1054.

Hansen, L. P., and Singleton, K. J. (1982). "Generalized Instrumental Variables Estimation of Nonlinear Rational Expectations Models." *Econometrica* 50(5), 1269–1286.

Harvey, D. I., Leybourne, S. J., and Newbold, P. (1998). "Tests for Forecast Encompassing." *Journal of Business & Economic Statistics* 16(2), 254–259.

Hausman, J. A. (1978). "Specification Tests in Econometrics." *Econometrica* 46(6), 1251–1272.

Hendricks, K., and Porter, R. H. (1988). "An Empirical Study of an Auction with Asymmetric Information." *American Economic Review* 78(5), 865–883.

Hendry, D. F. (1984). "Monte Carlo Experimentation in Econometrics." In Z. Griliches and M. D. Inteligaor (eds.), *Handbook of Econometrics*, Vol. 2, Amsterdam: North-Holland.

Hendry, D. F. (1995). *Dynamic Econometrics, Advanced Texts in Econometrics*, Granger C. W. J. and G. E. Mizon (eds.). Oxford: Oxford University Press.

Hendry, D. F., and Doornik, J. A. (2014). *Empirical Model Discovery and Theory Evaluation – Automatic Selection Methods in Econometrics*. Cambridge, MA: MIT Press.

Hendry, D. F., and Ericsson, N. R. (1991). "Modeling the Demand for Narrow Money in the United Kingdom and the United States." *European Economic Review* 35(4), 833–881 (with discussion).

Hendry, D. F., and Richard, J. F. (1982). "On the Formulation of Empirical Models in Dynamic Econometrics." *Journal of Econometrics* 20(1), 3–33.

Hendry, D. F., and Richard, J. F. (1989). "Recent Developments in the Theory of Encompassing." In B. Cornet and H. Tulkens (eds.), *Contribution to Operation Research and Economics*. Cambridge, MA: MIT Press, 393–440.

Hendry, D. F., Marcellino, M., and Mizon, G. E. (2008). "Guest Editors' Introduction to Special Issue on Encompassing." *Oxford Bulletin of Economics and Statistics* 70(s1), 715–719.

Inoue, A., and Kilian, L. (2006). "On the Selection of Forecasting Models." *Journal of Econometrics* 130(2), 273–306.

Keane, M. P. (1994). "A Computationally Practical Simulation Estimator for Panel Data." *Econometrica* 62(1), 95–116.

Krishna, V. (2010). *Auction Theory*, 2nd ed. Cambridge: Academic Press.

Kullback, S., and Leibler, R. A. (1951). "On Information and Sufficiency." *Annals of Mathematical Statistics* 22(1), 79–86.

Lakatos, I. (1978). *The Methodology of Scientific Research Programmes*, Vol. 1. J. Worrall and G. Currie, (eds.). Cambridge, MA: Cambridge University Press.

LeCam, L. (1964). "Sufficiency and Approximate Sufficiency." *Annals of Mathematical Statistics* 35(4), 1419–1455.

Lee, B., and Ingram, B. F. (1991). "Simulation Estimation of Time-Series Models." *Journal of Econometrics* 47(2-3), 197-205.

Liesenfeld, R., and Richard, J.-F. (2008). "Simulation Techniques for Panels: Efficient Importance Sampling." In L. Mátyás and P. Sevestre (eds.), *The Econometrics of Panel Data: Fundamentals and Recent Developments in Theory and Practice*, 3rd ed., Chvs 13.3.5 (Chapter 13), Mátyás, L. and P. Sevestre (eds.), Boston, Kluwer, 419–450.

Lu, M., Mizon, G. E., and Monfardini, C. (2008). "Simulation Encompassing: Testing Non-nested Hypotheses." *Oxford Bulletin of Economics and Statistics* 70(s1), 781–806.

Marshall, R. C., and Marx, L. (2007). "Bidder Collusion." *Journal of Economic Theory* 133(1), 374–402.

Marshall, R. C., and Marx, L. (2009). "The Vulnerability of Auctions to Bidder Collusion." *Quarterly Journal of Economics* 124(2), 883–910.

Marshall, R. C., and Marx, L. (2012). *The Economics of Collusion: Cartels and Bidding Rings*. Cambridge, MA: MIT Press.

McFadden, D. L. (1989). "A Method of Simulated Moments for Estimation of Discrete Response Models Without Numerical Integration." *Econometrica* 57(5), 995–1026.

McFadden, D. L., and Ruud, P. A. (1994). "Estimation by Simulation." *Review of Economics and Statistics* 76(4), 591–608.

Mizon, G. E. (1984). "The Encompassing Approach in Econometrics." In D. F. Hendry and K. F. Wallis (eds.), *Econometrics and Quantitative Economics*, Chapter 6, Oxford, UK: Basil Blackwell.

Mizon, G. E., and Hendry, D. F. (1980). "An Empirical Application and Monte Carlo Analysis of Tests of Dynamic Specifications." *Review of Economic Studies* 47(1), 21–45.

Mizon, G. E., and Richard, J. F. (1986). "The Encompassing Principle and Its Application to Testing Non-nested Hypotheses." *Econometrica* 54(3), 657–678.

Newey, W. K. (1985). "Maximum Likelihood Specification Testing and Conditional Moment Tests." *Econometrica* 53(5), 1047–1070.

Newey, W. K., and McFadden, D. L. (1994). "Large Sample Estimation and Hypothesis Testing." In R. F. Engle and D. L. McFadden (eds.), *Handbook of Econometrics*, Vol. 4, 2111–2145. Amsterdam, North-Holland.

Pagan, A. (2003). "Report on Modelling and Forecasting at the Bank of England," *Bank of England Quarterly Bulletin*, Spring, 60–88.

Pakes, A., and Pollard, D. (1989). "Simulation and the Asymptotics of Optimization Estimators." *Econometrica* 57(5), 1027–1057.

Pesaran, M. H. (1974). "On the General Problem of Model Selection." *Review of Economic Studies* 41(2), 153–171.

Pesaran, M. H., and Deaton, A. S. (1978). "Testing Non-Nested Nonlinear Regression Models." *Econometrica* 46(3), 677–694.

Popper, K. R. (1963). *Conjectures and Refutations*. London: Routledge & Kegan Paul.

Porter, R. H., and Zona, D. J. (1993). "Detection of Bid Rigging in Procurement Auctions." *Journal of Political Economy* 101(3), 518–538.

Porter, R. H., and Zona, D. J. (1999). "Ohio School Milk Markets: An Analysis of Bidding." *RAND Journal of Economics* 30(2), 263–288.

Press, W. H., Teukolsky, S. A., Vetterling, W. T., and Flannery, B. P. (2020). *Numerical Recipes*, Chapter 7, (3rd edition). Cambridge: Cambridge University Press.

Racine, J. (2000). "Consistent Cross-validatory Model-selection for Dependent data: hv-block Cross-validation." *Journal of Econometrics* 99(1), 39–61.

Richard, J. F. (1996). "Simulation Techniques." In L. Mátyás and P. Sevestre (eds.), *The Econometrics of Panel Data: Handbook of Theory and Application*, 2nd ed., Chapter 23, Boston: Kluwer.

Rubinstein, R. Y. (1981). *Simulations and the Monte Carlo Method*. New York: John Wiley & Sons.

Schurter, K. (2020). "Identification and Inference in First-Price Auctions with Collusion." Penn State Economics Working Paper. http://personal.psu.edu/kes380/files/FPAcollusion.pdf.

Shao, J. (1993). "Linear Model Selection by Cross-Validation." *Journal of the American Statistical Association* 88(422), 486–494.

Smith, A. (1993). "Estimating Nonlinear Time Series Models Using Simulated Vector Autoregressions." *Journal of Applied Econometrics* 8(S1), S63–S85.

Spanos, A., Hendry, D. F., and Reade, J. J. (2008). "Linear vs. Log-linear Unit-Root Specification: An Application of Mis-specification Encompassing." *Oxford Bulletin of Economics and Statistics* 70(s1), 829–847.

Tauchen, G.F (1985). "Diagnostic Testing and Evaluation of Maximum Likelihood Models." *Journal of Econometrics* 30(1–2), 415–443.

Theil, H. (1957). "Specification Errors and the Estimation of Economic Relationships." *Review of the International Statistical Institute* 25(1/3), 41–51.

Theil, H. (1961). *Economic Forecasts and Policy*, Amsterdam, North Holland.

van Dijk, H. K., Monfort, A., and Brown, B. W. (eds.), (1995). *Econometric Inference using Simulation Techniques*. Chichester, UK: John Wiley and Sons.

White, H. (1987). "Specification Testing in Dynamic Models." In T. F. Bewley, (ed.), *Advanced in Eonometrics*, 1–58. Cambridge: Cambridge University Press.

White, H. (2000). *Asymptotic Theory for Econometricians*. Revised ed. Orlando: Academic Press.

White, H., and Domowitz, I. (1984). "Nonlinear Regression with Dependent Observations." *Econometrica* 52(1), 143–161.

Wooldridge, J. M. (1990). "An Encompassing Approach to Conditional Mean Tests with Applications to Testing Nonnested Hypotheses." *Journal of Econometrics* 45(3), 331–350.

Index

Publisher contact:
The MIT Press
Massachusetts Institute of Technology
77 Massachusetts Avenue, Cambridge, MA 02139
mitpress.mit.edu

EU Authorised Representative:
Easy Access System Europe, Mustamäe tee 50,
10621 Tallinn, Estonia
gpsr.requests@easproject.com

Printed by Integrated Books International,
United States of America